Forgiveness

THE KEY TO DIVINE RELEASE

Dr. Alfred S. Cockfield

Foreword by Rev. Dennis A. Dillon

A *Christian times* PUBLICATION
NEW YORK

FORGIVENESS
The Key to Divine Release

Second Printing: March 2017

Published by

Christian times
PUBLICATIONS

718.638.6397
ChristianTimesPublications@gmail.com

Copyright © 1995 by Alfred Cockfield

All rights reserved. This book is protected under the copyright laws of the United States of America. This book may not be copied or reprinted for commercial gain or profit. The use of short quotations or occasional page copying for personal or group study is permitted and encouraged. Permission will be granted upon request.

Unless otherwise identified, Scripture quotations are from the King James Version of the Bible. Scripture quotations marked NIV are from the New International Version.

Take note that the name satan and related names are not capitalzied. We choose not to acknowledge him, even to the point of violating grammatical rules.

Printed in the United States of America

Library of Congress Cataloging-in-Publication Data
Cockfield, Alfred
FORGIVENESS: The Key to Divine Release
ISBN 978-0-9668730-4-7
1. Spirituality/Inspirational

Cover design by Karen Cox

Dedication

This book is dedicated to the two ladies in my life who have encouraged me, believed in me, supported me, and shared with me their love:
my wife, Linette,
and
my daughter, Barbara.

Also, to my son, Alfred II, my father, George, and my siblings, John, Simon, Sandra, David, George, and Paul; in memory of my mother, Caroline Kendall-Evans Cockfield; and the staff and congregation of God's Battalion of Prayer Church for allowing me to minister in the midst of my humanness.

I am grateful to the Lord that in His infinite wisdom, He coordinated our lives to come together as His body to accomplish His purpose on the earth.

Contents

Foreword vii

Preface xi

Introduction xiii

01   Forgiveness and the Model Prayer in Matthew 1

02   The Model Prayer in Luke 9

03   Aspects of Forgiveness 17

04   Forgiveness and Restoration 25

05   Wives, Forgive Your Husbands 29

06   Husbands, Forgive Your Wives 45

07   Parents, Children, and Forgiveness 57

08   Forgiving Family Members: Fathers and Stepfathers 71

09   Forgiving Family Members: Your Mother 83

10   Forgiving Family Members: Brothers and Sisters 91

11   Forgiving Your Pastor 105

12   Forgiveness and the Church 117

13   Forgiving Teachers and Educators 131

14   Forgivess and Your Job 145

15   Forgiving Your Friends 157

16   Forgiving Those From a Different Race 167

17   The Right Choice 191

Foreword

I believe it was **Dr. Martin Luther King, Jr.** who once said, "Let no one pull you low enough to hate them." And indeed, hate is low! Hate is the big brother of unforgiveness, and the two are like tormenting twins that haul you into a dungeon of resentment, malice, bitterness, and cynicism, and leave you there locked away with a heart brewing with pain and displeasure. You will need love and forgiveness to unlock those chains, swing those bars open, and pull you out of there.

Forgiveness is liberating, and it uplifts. It frees the heart from hate, liberates the mind from its evil thoughts of revenge, and it lifts the soul to the pinnacle of love.

As I read the pages of "Forgiveness: The Key to Divine Release," I sense a freedom in my soul. To forgive truly sets the prisoner free; and as we fully comprehend the power of forgiveness, we are awakened to that greater understanding that the forgiver is far more liberated than the forgiven.

Dr. Alfred Cockfield meticulously guides his readers with an easy-to-understand expository breakdown of the scriptures in his step-by-step formula for forgiveness. Within the confines of this manual are nuggets that, when applied, will lead to lasting peace and true security and safety in relationships. It outlines the many aspects of forgiveness, how forgiveness leads to restoration, how to forgive, why we should forgive, the dangers of unforgiveness, and the lasting blessings and benefits of a life marinated in the ingredients of love. As the author so skillfully conveys, when love is at the center, forgiveness is the automatic end result. "Forgiveness adds potency to our prayers and releases the fountain of love," you will soon read.

As he winds his way through the 17-chapter compendium of this very pertinent subject, Dr. Cockfield passionately connects the core areas and speaks to where forgiveness matters most: husbands and wives, families, churches and, of course, race relations. "Forgiveness is at the core of our human relationships," he explains.

As you read, I am confident of your satisfaction and fulfillment. Discover that forgiveness is not an exception – it's an expectation. Discover that praying without forgiving is like driving a car without wheels. Discover that forgiveness does not excuse the other person's behavior – it just prevents their action from destroying your heart. Discover that after a strong person says, "I am sorry," it's the stronger person that says, "You are forgiven."

With great wisdom and keen understanding, Dr. Alfred Cockfield paints a splendid mural of Divine forgiveness – but not with a big brush; he uses a roller to truly authenticate a vivid view of the God-kind of forgiveness that progresses to the heart. The heart will then release the offender's offense by refusing to allow such pain to take up permanent residence that could lower the offended to the prison of hate. Like King said, "Let no man pull you so low."

– Rev. Dennis A. Dillon
The New York Christian Times

Preface

When the disciples asked Jesus to teach them to pray, they had no idea what true prayer was. After Jesus gave them the proper elements of true prayer, they still did not quite comprehend the importance of these simple yet powerful words. In fact, the point they seemed to miss was the most important one: True prayer begins with a willingness to forgive.

The events surrounding the life and ministry of the disciples confirm their ignorance of the importance of forgiveness.

Forgiveness adds potency to prayer and releases the fountain of love toward the one to whom forgiveness is directed. I believe that when we begin to understand the importance of forgiveness and make it a part of our daily life, these words of Jesus will be applied to us: "By this shall all men know that ye are My disciples, if ye have love one to another" (Jn. 13:35).

I have heard and read many sermons and teachings centered around the Lord's Prayer. What I want to share in this book in no way diminishes the teachings of the Holy Spirit that have come through His servants. Their inspiration is a part of the whole. This book, though, is written for one purpose: that by the grace of God, as you read each chapter, you would look inwardly and honestly examine your efforts to deal with and apply forgiveness in your life. Remember, we are forgiven by God through the Lord Jesus Christ as we forgive those who have sinned against us.

Introduction

The desire to pen this book began as a seed planted in my heart. I was first aware of this desire as I was preparing a speech to be delivered in February, 1993, at Harbor Front in Toronto, Canada. I was offered the opportunity to speak as part of a Black History Month celebration.

Books that I'd read decades ago became relevant as I began to refresh my mind on Black history. One of those books, *The Challenge of the Congo* by the late Dr. Kawame Nkrumah, focused on the atrocities committed against the Black race. As I struggled to recall the details of Dr. Nkrumah's book, the Holy Spirit whispered to my soul: "Forgive them as your Father which is in Heaven has forgiven you." My spirit was suddenly renewed and the contrary spirit of hate that was seeking a place in my heart had to depart as the love of God began to reign. It was at this point that the Holy Spirit nudged me to look deeper into the many aspects of forgiveness.

As I began my study, I learned that forgiveness is not just sweeping things under the mat. Rather, it is facing those persons or situations head-on, and after looking at the problem for what it is, forgiving the person or persons who have wronged you.

When you address a problem while it is fresh, you know exactly the reason for your forgiveness. If the hurt is too great, pray until you can truly forgive and forget because the forgiveness you seek from God is tied to releasing those who have sinned against you. When you can sincerely forgive, then you can pray for the Kingdom of God to be made known to all men. It is forgiveness that demonstrates our love for one another.

Forgiveness is at the core of human relationships. It is also at the center of our spiritual relationships. As we forgive horizontally, we are forgiven vertically. If I refuse to extend my hand outward to my fellow man, God will not extend His hand downward to me. So forgiveness first of all requires me to deal with myself. Then I am required to extend forgiveness to those close to me—father, mother, brother, sister, uncle, and aunt.

Finally, I am required to reach beyond my family to my teacher, pastor, church, brothers and sisters in the church, boss, and co-workers. Eventually, I am required to forgive every person with whom I come in contact, if he hurts me.

Only if you were never born would you be exempt from the necessity to forgive. You live in a real world made up of real people. People hurt people both by commission and by omission; by being too friendly or not friendly enough. Since you were born and since you must live your life among people here on earth, you need to read this book. You will learn something about forgiveness that you can put into practice. Then as you practice forgiveness, you will be blessed, and your life will be filled with peace and love.

Dr. Alfred S. Cockfield

Chapter 1

Forgiveness and the Model Prayer in Matthew

The prayer that Jesus taught in His Sermon on the Mount in Matthew 6, the Lord's Prayer, is a model for all prayer.

This same prayer was included in Luke 11. There is no indication why Mark and John chose not to include the prayer in their writings and, unfortunately, this leaves us without their comments or perspective. We can only assume that the Holy Spirit wanted Mark and John to concentrate on other matters.

Luke tells us that the disciples were observing Jesus in prayer when they asked Him to teach them how to pray. They had seen the disciples of John the Baptist follow his teaching on prayer; they wanted to

Forgiveness: The Key to Divine Release

follow their Master's teachings too. Although the Scriptures do not provide us with a type of John the Baptist's prayer, we do have a record of some prayers from the Old and New Testaments that deal with the subject of forgiveness. A good example is Solomon's prayer of dedication in First Kings 8.

There must have been something inspiring or unique about Jesus' prayer because it compelled one of His disciples to ask Jesus to teach them to pray. Since they had learned to pray as John the Baptist prayed, we can conclude they knew how to talk to God through prayer. Usually the children of Israel prayed using the formula of the God of Abraham, Isaac, and Jacob. In this type of prayer they approached the Lord as the God of the covenant between Him and Israel. In this way they relied on Him to act in good faith to the covenant and help them in times of need or trouble. This type of prayer is relevant while the petitioner is ignorant of God's commands, but now God commands all men everywhere to repent of their ignorance and seek Him at the throne of His grace.

From the way Matthew placed the prayer in his Gospel, and based on what Jesus said immediately following it, I believe Jesus is showing us that true prayer originates from the heart of man, not from the formulas or traditions of the elders. If we begin with Matthew 5:37, we see Jesus' teaching progressing

Forgiveness and the Model Prayer in Matthew

from the legal injunctions to a much higher dimension. The following is my paraphrase of Matthew 5:37-42:

"But let your communication [*heart relation*] be yea, yea; or nay, nay; for whatever is more than these comes of evil. You have heard that it had been said, an eye for an eye and a tooth for a tooth [*legal position*], but I say unto you that you resist not evil [*legal fighting*] or legal position, but rather, I want you to rise to a higher state of being." So Jesus says, "But whoever shall smite you on the right cheek, turn to him the other also. And if any man will sue at the law and take away your coat, let him have your cloak also. And whoever shall compel you to go a mile, go with him two. Give to him who asks you, and from him who would borrow of you do not turn away."

Jesus continues to teach the higher laws in Matthew 5:43-48. Again, I provide my own paraphrase:

"You have heard that it had been said, you shall love your neighbor and hate your enemy or [*love the one who is good to you, which is Christ's definition of a neighbor in the parable of the Good Samaritan, and hate the one who is not kind*]; but I say unto you, love your enemies, bless those who hate you, and pray for those who despitefully use you and persecute you, that you may be sons of your Father, who

Forgiveness: The Key to Divine Release

is in heaven; for He makes His sun to rise on the evil and the good, and sends rain on the just and on the unjust. For if you love those who love you, what reward do you have? Do not even the tax collectors the same? And if you greet your brethren only, what do you more than others? Do not even the heathen so? Be therefore perfect even as your Father who is in heaven is perfect."

In this teaching on the heart of God, Jesus teaches the way of life for one whose heart is like His Father's.

"Take heed that you do not your alms before men, to be seen by them; otherwise you have no reward of your Father who is in heaven. Therefore when you do your alms, do not sound a trumpet before you, or make a noise in the streets; but let it be a genuine heart decision because you are imitating your heavenly Father who will reward you as you cultivate a heart of forgiveness and genuine love" (Matthew 6:1-2, my paraphrase).

Jesus also emphasizes that the Father looks at the heart before He listens to what we have to say.

"But you, when you pray, enter into your closet or your secret place where no human can see you after you close the door behind you. Nevertheless, your Father who sees the hidden

Forgiveness and the Model Prayer in Matthew

things or sees in secret shall hear what you pray for and if your heart is without ought against anyone, He will reward you openly" (Matthew 6:6, my paraphrase).

As a matter of fact, He says we do not need to pray over and over again about the same matter because God is our Father and He knows what we have need of, even before we ask Him (see Matthew 6:7-8).

It is at this very point that the Holy Spirit inspired Matthew to include the Lord's Prayer. To understand the importance of this placement, we must look back to Jesus' teachings in Matthew 5:37-42.

First, Jesus pointed out that we are not called to resist evil or to live according to legal principles. Instead, God has called every Christian to live in the Spirit. No longer must we seek an eye for an eye and a tooth for a tooth. God is in charge of our lives, and He will take care of us so we can go the extra mile.

Secondly, in verses 43-48, He says that we are not like the people of the world who love only those who love them and hate those who hate them. We must be imitators of the One who loved us while we were yet sinners. He loved us even before we became sinners, and demonstrated His love through Jesus Christ, the Lamb slain before the foundation of the earth. God forgave man before man sinned. Adam did not surprise God when he disobeyed and ate fruit from the tree of the knowledge of good and evil. Still after

Forgiveness: The Key to Divine Release

Adam sinned, God returned to offer him a way to be fully restored.

Thirdly, in Matthew 6:1-4 we are instructed not to do things because we want to be seen or praised by men. That is the way the heathen behave. We are to act differently.

Finally, we are reminded that God is not impressed by long public prayers that spring from a heart filled with wrong motives (see Mt. 6:5-8). Instead, the Father is looking for sincere prayer that stems from sincere motives and a sincere heart. That is why Jesus tells us to enter into our room, close the door, and pray to our Father in secret. Then, our Father who sees in secret will reward us openly.

When you can pray in this way, you can follow the model of prayer that Jesus outlined. You will see the qualities of your heavenly Father in yourself. You will also experience a sense of freedom and confidence as the Spirit prays through you. Boldly you can come to the throne and say, "Our Father which art in heaven...." The "our" speaks of togetherness. You cannot come to God when you are not right with a brother or sister and say "Our Father." If you do, you are excluding someone from the "our" that begins the prayer. To say "our" means you include all of us. God, who is in Heaven, is the Father of us all and His name is hallowed. His Kingdom has come. Let the rule of God come into your life and let His rule be

Forgiveness and the Model Prayer in Matthew

carried out on earth as it is in Heaven. Whatever He decrees in Heaven is active on earth and is applied by those who are members of His Kingdom.

We look to God for our daily provision. It is not His will that we go hungry or naked. Before He made man He planted a garden in which every need of man was supplied. Since God is the One who has made us and provides everything we need, we should not find it so difficult to forgive those who sinned against us. After all, we receive God's forgiveness when we repent of our sins and call upon Christ.

Although we should not, we often make statements like these: "I will forgive but I will not forget"; "I have to think about that"; "It is too much for me to forgive"; "I forgive you, but I will keep you at arm's length"; or "I will feed you with a long spoon." There are still other clichés that we use to try to keep our conscience quiet while we disobey God's directive to forgive those who sinned against us. Remember, the disciples also had a hard time with forgiveness.

Do you have an option not to forgive? Yes, you do. You can certainly choose not to forgive. But you should also understand the consequences of such a choice. Do you want to be in fellowship with God or not? If your fellowship with God is not important to you, then you do not have to forgive those who have sinned against you. However, if you consider your fellowship with God and your eternal destiny to be vital, then you must learn to forgive those who have sinned against you.

Forgiveness: The Key to Divine Release

Jesus did not end His model prayer at this juncture—lest we feel that we are the ones who live a righteous life. Jesus brings to light that we are miserable failures and deserving of nothing. If left to our own devices, we would miss the blessings of God and the gift of eternal life in His presence. Thank God for His grace and His favor that He offers even though we do not deserve it. Because of His mercy and grace, we can ask Him not to lead us "into temptation, but deliver us from evil" (Mt. 6:13).

Without the love and faithfulness of God, we would all be cast away. Yet the rule of God will not come to us if our hearts are not cleansed from unforgiveness.

"For if we forgive men their trespasses or sins, our heavenly Father will also forgive us. But if we do not forgive men their trespasses, neither will our Father forgive our trespasses" (Matthew 6:14-15, my paraphrase).

Chapter 2

The Model Prayer in Luke

Now it came to pass, as they went, that He entered into a certain village: and a certain woman named Martha received Him into her house. And she had a sister called Mary, who also sat at Jesus' feet, and heard His word. But Martha was cumbered about much serving, and came to Him, and said, Lord, dost Thou not care that my sister hath left me to serve alone? bid her therefore that she help me. And Jesus answered and said unto her, Martha, Martha, thou art careful and troubled about many things: but one thing is needful: and Mary hath chosen that good part, which shall not be taken away from her (Luke 10:38-42).

In Luke's Gospel narration, the Lord's model prayer follows the story of Jesus' visit to the home of

Forgiveness: The Key to Divine Release

Martha and Mary. In that story we see Martha's concern was directed toward physical or material concerns. Such matters are mainly temporal. Because she expressed these concerns to Jesus, I am led to believe that she was seeking approval or recognition. So many times we honestly believe that God is pleased with the things we spend time on rather than the things He has asked us to do. Martha was not the first person who believed the Lord would be satisfied with what she chose to do, instead of with what He required of her. This theme is consistent throughout the Bible.

For example, Adam chose to eat fruit from the tree of the knowledge of good and evil, which was forbidden to him, while he ignored the tree of life, which was available to him. We also have the example of his son Cain. Cain chose to give God what he wanted (produce from the earth), instead of what God required (a lamb). Because he was not a herdsman, he would have had to buy a lamb. It would have cost him something to obey God. Because he was unwilling to obey, his offering was rejected by God. In the end he lost his home and family and was marked for his actions against God and his brother.

When it comes to obeying God, Martha, Adam, and Cain are not so different from us today. We want to be accepted and blessed by God on our terms. Jesus pointed out to Martha that Mary made the right choice, a choice that would be with her forever.

10

The Model Prayer in Luke

I believe the Holy Spirit chose to record the Lord's Prayer in Luke's Gospel after the story of Martha and Mary to show us the importance of choice in the order of prayer. When we pray, we are choosing or setting our priorities down in front of God. We want God to hear our prayer and respond. According to the Lord's Prayer, if we do not forgive those who have sinned against us, neither will our heavenly Father forgive us.

Immediately following the Lord's Prayer, Luke inserts the parable of the persistent friend (verses 5-8 in Luke 11). Does this have any relevance to the Lord's Prayer and forgiveness? I believe it does. How could someone be your friend if there is something in your heart against him? You would hardly go out of your way for someone you have not forgiven.

Which of you would go to a friend at midnight and say, "Friend, lend me three loaves of bread, for another friend of mine has just come to visit. He is on a journey and I am without bread. I do not have anything to give him to eat." Suppose your friend refuses to get out of bed and help you? If there is nothing in your heart against him, you might persist and insist that he should get out of bed, open the door and give you the bread you need. Because of your persistence and friendship, he will answer your request and help you out.

Forgiving someone who has hurt us is not easy, but we must realize the importance of having a clean

Forgiveness: The Key to Divine Release

heart before our heavenly Father and our fellowman. In the same way this man was persistent in his appeal for bread, we too must be persistent to forgive those who have hurt us. They need our forgiveness and we need to forgive them. Even though it is difficult, we must look to the Holy Spirit to enable us to forgive, whether it is our father, mother, brother, sister, pastor, church member, boss, coworker, friend, society, a different race, or whoever.

So many times I have heard people say, "I could have helped him. But because of what he did to me, I am not going out of my way to help him. Normally I would help—but if I have to go out of my way, you can forget it. Not me! If it was anybody else, I would gladly do it." Does that sound familiar? It is quite evident that unforgiveness causes us to be unlike our heavenly Father when He has called us to be like Him. To have an unforgiving spirit is to grieve the heart of God, who is always willing to forgive us when we ask Him to.

As a Christian, I know people who attend services of fasting and prayer every time they are announced at church. These people are willing to give up eating for a day. If they are asked to make some sacrifice for the ministry, they don't hesitate. They are willing to do anything they are asked, as long as they don't have to interact with a "certain individual." Too many Christians are like Martha, willing to sacrifice their

The Model Prayer in Luke

time and energy, to speak with the tongues of angels, to give to charity, or to do anything that is asked of them at church, but still refusing to forgive the one who has hurt them.

We should consider the times we have hurt our heavenly Father. Don't we expect Him to forgive us each time we ask? God is always faithful to forgive us and to cleanse us from all unrighteousness (see 1 Jn. 1:9). We also want Him to free us from our sin while we insist on holding someone else in bondage to our unforgiveness.

Therefore is the kingdom of heaven likened unto a certain king, which would take account of his servants. And when he had begun to reckon, one was brought unto him, which owed him ten thousand talents. But forasmuch as he had not to pay, his lord commanded him to be sold, and his wife, and children, and all that he had, and payment to be made. The servant therefore fell down, and worshipped him, saying, Lord, have patience with me, and I will pay thee all. Then the lord of that servant was moved with compassion, and loosed him, and forgave him the debt. But the same servant went out, and found one of his fellowservants, which owed him an hundred pence: and he laid hands on him, and took him by the throat, saying, Pay me that thou owest. And his fellowservant fell down at his feet, and besought him,

Forgiveness: The Key to Divine Release

saying, Have patience with me, and I will pay thee all. And he would not: but went and cast him into prison till he should pay the debt. So when his fellowservants saw what was done, they were very sorry, and came and told unto their lord all that was done. Then his lord, after that he had called him, said unto him, O thou wicked servant, I forgave thee all that debt, because thou desiredst me: shouldest not thou also have had compassion on thy fellowservant, even as I had pity on thee? And his lord was wroth, and delivered him to the tormentors, till he should pay all that was due unto him. So likewise shall My heavenly Father do also unto you, if ye from your hearts forgive not every one his brother their trespasses (Matthew 18:23-35).

This man, whose master forgave him of a huge debt, left his master's house debt-free and immediately refused to forgive a man who owed him a few pennies. Jesus made it perfectly clear that forgiveness is not an option for a Christian. Through this parable He spells out the principles of the Kingdom of Heaven. We, like this servant, owe a great debt. In this parable the debt is expressed in terms of money. He owed 10,000 talents and was himself owed 10 pence. Today his debt, in dollars, would be $9.6 million, while the debt he refused to forgive was about $16. This unforgiving man went even further when he grabbed the debtor by the throat. The extent of

The Model Prayer in Luke

his unforgiving spirit was displayed when the other man, kneeling at his feet and begging for mercy, was cast into prison. What the unforgiving servant did not count on was those who would tell his master of his actions. Once his master found out how mean-spirited his servant was toward the poor debtor, he restored the previous debt and required his servant to pay it all.

Like the children of Israel, I believe Christians assume that either God does not see or He does not care how we respond to those who need our forgiveness. Jesus is teaching us, through this parable, that forgiveness is based on our willingness to forgive those in need of forgiveness. For the servant, the choice was to forgive or to live the rest of his life in debt and torment. When the master heard of his servant's actions, the master said, "O thou wicked servant, I forgave thee all that debt, because thou desiredst me! Shouldest not thou also have had compassion on thy fellowservant, even as I had pity on thee?" The master was greatly disappointed and became angry. He then treated his servant the way the servant treated his fellowservant. In concluding this parable, Jesus said, "So likewise shall My heavenly Father do also unto you, if ye from your hearts forgive not every one his brother their trespasses."

It is important to consider the phrase "from your hearts." Many hold to a philosophy that says, "I

Forgiveness: The Key to Divine Release

might forgive you but I will never forget what you have done." If you forgive from your heart, why would you waste time and energy remembering what a person has done? In the first place, if you continue to remember, you probably still have something in your heart against that person. Secondly, you are building a platform for the devil to work from there in your heart. He'll keep reminding you why you should not go the extra mile for that person: "You remember what he did last year. He hasn't changed; he'll do the same thing again. Maybe, if you give him a chance, he will do worse than that to you. Don't trust him, ever." Meanwhile, you look at the person and smile to make him believe there is nothing between you. When you forgive from the heart you will go the extra mile, knowing that you are in obedience to the Word of God.

I have sinned many times, but my heavenly Father has not given up on me. He still forgives and forgets. I cannot tell you how many times He has forgiven me and buried my sins in the sea of forgetfulness, after removing them as far as the east is from the west. Men have gone to both the North Pole and South Pole, but I have never heard of someone going to the end of the east or the west. God removes sins so far that it is impossible to bring them back. Even as God has done to you, so you must do to those who sinned against you.

Chapter 3

Aspects of Forgiveness

The Need to Forgive

The need to forgive a person, even though he has wronged you, is vital for releasing the power of God in the midst of His Church. Forgiving also is not an act to be taken lightly. Therefore, Jesus offers a three-step formula to keep unforgiveness from remaining among the brethren.

Step 1. If a brother or sister sins against you, go to that individual personally and tell him or her what he or she did. If the person hears you and asks your forgiveness, then you must forgive. Now, you may think, "If he knows he has wronged me, why must I go to him?" It may be that the person does not realize he has offended you. Sometimes people do

Forgiveness: The Key to Divine Release

things as a joke and have no idea that you found their actions offensive until you go to them and tell them why you were offended.

Another reason I must go to my brother and tell him his fault is that, even though he might be well aware that he has offended me, he may be too ashamed or afraid to come to me. By going to him and raising the issue, he can face the situation and admit his error. This will clear the air between us and move us both forward into harmony.

A third reason to confront the offender is Jesus' commandment for us to go. Once there is a problem, it must be resolved. Jesus gives an imperative: "Moreover if thy brother shall trespass against thee, go and tell him his fault between thee and him alone: if he shall hear thee, thou hast gained thy brother" (Mt. 18:15). I can hear the next question before you even think it: "What if he does not hear me?" Then you take step number 2.

Step 2. Take one or more witnesses with you when you return to your brother (Mt. 18:16). Sometimes a person might try to avoid an issue by attempting to make light of your reason for coming to him, but when you return with two or three witnesses, he will realize you are serious. He might quickly change his attitude and resolve the issue. Your words will be established by the presence of those two or three witnesses. Even then the offender may still be stubborn. You might think, "What if he still refuses to hear and respond?" Jesus tells you to go on to step three.

Step 3. If he refuses to respond in front of two or three witnesses, bring the matter to the whole church (see Mt. 18:17). Every believer must submit to some level of authority. If he refuses to hear the person he has wronged, then he must be given a second chance to right the wrong in the presence of witnesses. If he rejects that opportunity, then he is brought to the church to see if he will submit to the authority of the assembly. Should he refuse to submit to the assembly, Jesus says he is not part of the body and should be treated as an outsider.

Binding and Loosing

Verily I say unto you, Whatsoever ye shall bind on earth shall be bound in heaven: and whatsoever ye shall loose on earth shall be loosed in heaven (Matthew 18:18).

Our relationship on earth is registered in Heaven. That is why we pray "Thy will be done in earth, as it is in heaven" (Mt. 6:10). Heaven must affect us—if not, we will affect Heaven. For example, when you confront a person with a sin he has committed against you, you are helping to release him in Heaven. His account in Heaven is automatically frozen when he sins against you. It is similar to when a country is accused of transgressing against another

Forgiveness: The Key to Divine Release

country and the international community acts to freeze their assets in the first country. Until that country repents of its actions and makes the transgression right, it is deprived of its assets. Similarly, when someone sins against you, God freezes his account in Heaven until that person makes it right with you.

The steps that Jesus outlined to help a person keep his account active in Heaven are to keep God from being accused of unrighteousness. Therefore, you help God's Kingdom to operate on righteous principles. Heaven will freeze whatever is frozen on earth, and will release whatever is released on earth. If you do not fulfill Jesus' command to help a person keep a good account in Heaven, you are abusing heavenly principles and causing Him to freeze an account that could have been released to further the Kingdom of God. All you need to do is fulfill your obligation by following the three steps of restoration.

Sins bound on earth are bound in Heaven; sins released on earth are released in Heaven, to the glory of God and furtherance of the Kingdom of Heaven. Because nothing is between you and your brother, both of you have an open line to Heaven and are able to come boldly to the throne and find grace to help in your time of need.

If Two Shall Agree

Again I say unto you, That if two of you shall agree on earth as touching any thing that they shall ask, it shall be done for them of my Father which is in heaven (Matthew 18:19).

Look at the benefits you receive when you forgive. When you forgive your brother, you keep your account active. When you help that person see his fault, you also help keep his account in Heaven active. Thus two accounts that would have been frozen are kept open and working for the Kingdom of Heaven. Then, when you pray and agree with your brother or sister, your prayers produce rich dividends. Whatever you ask will be done. (See Matthew 18:19.) In addition, you will dwell in the presence of your Father who is in Heaven: "For where two or three are gathered together in My name, there am I in the midst of them" (Mt. 18:20).

In John 15:7 Jesus said, "If ye abide in Me, and My words abide in you, ye shall ask what ye will, and it shall be done unto you." In this text Jesus was teaching about bearing fruit. If you abide in Him and His words of forgiveness abide in you, you can pray the Lord of the harvest to send forth laborers (see Mt. 9:38).

The cry of pastors wherever I go is "Too few laborers!" So many pastors are on the verge of burnout. Let us forgive so we can agree in praying for laborers.

How Many Times Should You Forgive Your Brother?

I can imagine Peter saying to the Lord Jesus "Yes, Lord, I know all that You have said is true and

Forgiveness: The Key to Divine Release

wonderful. Yes, the benefits are truly great and well worth the fact that I should forgive my brother. All of that is good and I can agree with what You have said." Then with his eyes fixed on Jesus' lips, he continues, "But tell me, Lord, how often shall my brother sin against me, and I forgive him? Till seven times?" Jesus said unto him, "I don't say until seven times, but until seventy times seven." (See Matthew 18:21-22.)

I believe Peter was floored at Jesus' response. I am sure he thought he had it covered when he offered to forgive seven times. Forgiving seven times should be the limit for any person, but Jesus confronted him with a greater truth. In essence Jesus said, "Peter, you cannot forgive your brother enough times in your lifetime."

The things that people might do to you and the number of times they do them is very small in comparison to the many times and the type of sins you have sinned against God. Your sins are like the debt of the servant who was forgiven more than he could pay in his lifetime. In other words, I owed a debt I could not pay; He paid my debt though He did not owe it. I needed someone to forgive my sins so I could tell a brand new story, "Sins Forgiven." Even if you had to forgive your brother 490 times 16 dollars, it only equals 7,840 dollars. This is nowhere close to the debt you were forgiven.

It might seem hard or unfair to have to forgive your brother that many times. When you begin feeling that way, all you need to do is ask the Lord to give

Aspects of Forgiveness

you a vision of your past life. Then you can see how many times you sinned against Him before you got saved—and even after you got saved, how many times you failed Him. I am sure that with such a vision, you will have no difficulty in forgiving your brother 70 times 7.

The Kingdom operates on love between God and man. God so loved you that, while you were a sinner, sinning every day, Jesus Christ died on the cross to bring you forgiveness of sins. After you became a Christian, He provided a fresh supply of mercies each day so your failures can be forgiven before they are committed. (If that isn't love, then tell me what is.) You then, like Jesus, must love your brother and be ready to forgive him.

Love and forgiveness are interrelated. Love caused God to provide for your forgiveness; His love in you must cause you to forgive and love your brother, even when he sins against you more than once. Jesus spent a lot of time emphasizing the principle of love and forgiveness. If you fail to grasp the importance of it, you can be responsible for short-circuiting the Kingdom of Heaven on earth, to the point where it does not operate here as it operates in Heaven.

I believe that if Judas Iscariot had sought God's forgiveness when he had the opportunity, he would have been forgiven. God is more willing to forgive than man is willing to seek His forgiveness. Jesus dipped His hand in the dish with Judas as a sign of

Forgiveness: The Key to Divine Release

friendship. If at that point Judas had said, "Lord, I repent of my greed. I realize my greed will destroy me," I believe he would have found forgiveness and the scribes would have been forced to find another way to capture Jesus.

In His desire to reemphasize the importance of forgiveness, after stating that we must be willing to forgive 70 times 7, Jesus went on to give the parable that the Kingdom of Heaven is like a certain king who forgave one servant of a great amount who, in his turn, could not forgive another servant a very small amount.

Chapter 4

Forgiveness and Restoration

Forgiveness and Marriage

And He shall send Jesus Christ, which before was preached unto you: whom the heaven must receive until the times of restitution of all things, which God hath spoken by the mouth of all His holy prophets since the world began. For Moses truly said unto the fathers, A prophet shall the Lord your God raise up unto you of your brethren, like unto me; Him shall ye hear in all things whatsoever He shall say unto you (Acts 3:20-22).

The word that I would like us to focus on as we examine the issue of forgiving spouses is *restitution*. Peter, full of the Holy Spirit, included this word in his second address after the Day of Pentecost. According

Forgiveness: The Key to Divine Release

to the *World Book Dictionary*, this word means "to give back of that which has been lost or taken away; the act of making good any loss, damage, or injury: the return of an elastic body to its original form or position when released from strain; rebuild, replace, return, reparation, amends." [1]

It is clear that restitution means to restore something, to put it back into its original condition or shape. When Jesus ascended into Heaven, He was to remain there until the time of restitution of "all things." Do "all things" include the family structure? I believe that the family is near and dear to God's heart. It must be restored to its proper place and function.

At the core of the family is the relationship of the husband and the wife. The pressure on this relationship today is extreme. Demonic forces work day and night to bring about the destruction of what God has ordained between man and woman.

At the dawn of creation, God established this union as the basis for the development and expansion of His Kingdom on earth. After God created Adam, He took a rib from him and created Eve. Then He brought her to him, and Adam said, "...This is now bone of my bones, and flesh of my flesh: she shall be

---

1. *World Book Dictionary*, Doubleday & Company, Inc., 1987; World Book, Inc., Illinois, 1988.

Forgiveness and Restoration

called Woman, because she was taken out of Man. Therefore shall a man leave his father and his mother, and shall cleave unto his wife: and they shall be one flesh" (Gen. 2:23-24).

God's process of restoration is designed to take place in His Body, the Church. This is the one place in which marriage is held in honor and supported as God has ordained. Marriage is also designed to reflect or be an example of God's commitment to His Bride, the Church. This Bride is the one for whom Jesus will soon return to take away to His eternal Kingdom. Every time a marriage ends in divorce, it is a slap in God's face. Divorce makes it seem as if God did not know what He was doing when He blessed the union of man and woman. Unfortunately, we see an increasing number of marriages ending in divorce. If marriages here aren't working, how can we be certain it will work between Christ and His Church?

Many Christians have the opinion that it doesn't matter what happens while we are on earth because, when Christ comes, everything will be all right; we shall be like Him. I am not sure how far this truth can be stretched. The Scriptures tell us that those who endure to the end shall be saved (see Mt. 24:13). Seven times in Revelation, we are told that those who overcome will inherit all things. It is also true that salvation is God's free gift to those who believe

Forgiveness: The Key to Divine Release

in Jesus Christ (see Rom. 5:15). John's Gospel clearly states that to as many as receive Christ, God gives them power to become sons of God, even to them that believe on His name (see Jn. 1:12).

If we have been given power to become sons of God, then we must assume we have also been given the power to live as sons of God. Over the years, I have given serious thought to the marriage covenant. I am convinced that when God began to set up the whole plan of marriage, He had one thing in mind: marriage was designed for God's people, or for Christians. Marriage must be built on faith and trust. When it is, it reflects our relationship with God. Without faith, it is impossible to please God (see Heb. 11:6). Without faith in God and trust in a spouse, it is very difficult to have a true marriage—one that mirrors our relationship with the Lord Jesus Christ.

The restitution I speak of is for homes with both a father and a mother working together in a solid union. This union reflects the union between Christ and His Church, the union that gives us confidence in believing the Bridegroom is coming back for His Bride. In order for Christ to come, the Bride must make herself ready. As Christians, our walk with God is not always easy; many times we have failed our heavenly Bridegroom. But we are His Bride and every time we go to Him and ask His forgiveness, He has always been faithful and just to forgive us.

Chapter 5

Wives, Forgive Your Husbands

Forgiveness between a husband and wife is a necessary part of the restitution of "all things." Many homes have been destroyed because a wife refused to forgive a failing husband. The reasons are many. Sometimes two people live in the same house but lead separate lives. Sometimes they remain married while living in separate homes, without any contact with each other. What can cause the separation of two people who were once so close? The answer is unforgiveness.

If a wife is willing to forgive her husband his sin, her heavenly Father will also forgive her sins. But if she refuses to forgive her husband his sins, neither

Forgiveness: The Key to Divine Release

will her heavenly Father forgive her sins. Are you willing to live outside of God's forgiveness? No one can be happy in the state of unforgiveness. Therefore, the Lord wants wives to forgive their husbands of their sins. Forgiveness is the first step to a healthy marital relationship and the restoration of a broken union. God is seeking to restore and to put every marriage back the way it was at the beginning. People need to stop seeing their own little worlds and begin to see the greater picture.

Wives give a number of reasons for their inability to forgive their husbands. One couple came to me because the wife claimed she could not endure her husband any longer. She said she was better off without him. Finally, after all the huffing and puffing was over, I was able to get a question in. "What is your husband doing that has caused you to be so upset?" I asked. "Pastor!" she began in frustration, then after a pause, went on to say her husband had no idea of what went on in the home. He did not know when any of the bills were due or when they were paid. She had been doing all those things over the years and now she was tired of taking on all those responsibilities. Her husband, she said, was not concerned about any aspect of the business of the home.

I asked if he gave her money to pay the bills. She said that he gave her money weekly, which was fine. But she was frustrated because he did not know

Wives, Forgive Your Husbands

when bills were due. She felt that he needed to be involved in case she forgot or was unable to take care of paying them. I thought that made sense, so I asked her husband what he had to say about his wife's comments. He said, "Pastor, when we were first married, I did everything, but she was not satisfied. Nothing suited her, so I allowed her to have complete control. This seemed to make her very happy. All I had to do was work and give her my check. She took care of everything. Now since that is getting difficult for her to do, I have become public enemy number one."

Another woman came to me every week to complain about her husband. She spoke badly of him and described him as cheap and mean. He never gave her enough money for the children and household expenses. Her complaints continued until I met her husband. He told a different story and I realized that they did not understand each other. They had different agendas. Actually, he was faithful to give her money for the home and to help with the children. She worked too, but she was not willing to contribute any of her income toward their expenses. He felt she should make some level of contribution.

This condition continued and, eventually, escalated to the point of involving the children. Neither parent would give in to the other, allowing unforgiveness and bitterness to invade their relationship. The

Forgiveness: The Key to Divine Release

children then became pawns and were used as a means of communication between the couple. Before long, the whole family was polarized; some of the children took the father's side and some the mother's. The outcome was devastating to all concerned.

I arranged a meeting with both parties to take a fresh look at the situation. After a time of prayer, I pointed out that based upon the present situation, there had to be a change of attitude and a willingness to forgive. Otherwise they would lose their marriage, their testimony, their children, and all the things they had worked so hard to enjoy. After I had counseled the couple, I separated them so I could work with each one individually. I asked each to confirm my analysis of their relationship. Both agreed that my analysis was correct. Then I encouraged them to start afresh by forgiving each other.

The husband was willing to forgive his wife and, by the grace of God, make a fresh start to rebuild the relationship that had been destroyed. The wife, on the other hand, was unforgiving and unrelenting. She vowed that she would never forgive him and swore that she would see him destroyed. She was adamant in her refusal to forgive, ignoring God's warning that if she refused to forgive her husband, neither would her heavenly Father forgive her sins. She chose a course of destruction and an unjust judge to carry out her desires. She was determined to get the court to give her a large sum of money, but the unjust judge gave her less. She appealed, but did not succeed. So far as I know, she is still trying to get the court system to reconsider her plea.

I do not know who was advising her, but it is clear they were not advising her with wisdom from the Word of God. Because she was not willing to forgive her husband, her divorce petition was granted. Then she sued her husband for the house and everything in it. I do not know if she will succeed, but it seems the price she is willing to pay is too high. In the wake of her unforgiveness, she is leaving a broken home and children who will suffer emotionally, mentally, financially, and spiritually. How do I minister to children of parents who have gone their separate ways? How do I tell them that serving God makes a difference, when they have yet to see a difference in their own home? The most significant people in their lives, their mother and father, have set a terrible example, denying God's wisdom and choosing selfish pride over love and forgiveness. I know in my heart that unforgiveness has brought about the complete disintegration of this Christian family. In the end, they will have to answer God.

There is another situation I want to address—two women and one man. Often I hear some women say, "You have the wedding ring, but I have the man." In

Forgiveness: The Key to Divine Release

this case the husband is seldom, if ever, at home with his family. He seems to find fulfillment with someone other than his wife. Should he be forgiven?

Before I answer that question, I want to ask you to consider the word *forgiveness*. What does it really mean to forgive? According to *World Book Dictionary*, to forgive is: "(1) to give up the wish to punish or get even with; (2) not have hard feelings at or toward; and, (3) give up all claim to; not demand payments for: to err is human, to forgive, divine (Alexander Pope)."[1] In the case of a husband's unfaithfulness, what does a wife's forgiveness mean? Is World Book's definition adequate for you as a wife to sincerely forgive your husband? The answer could be both "yes" and "no."

According to the Scriptures, marriage is the joining of two lives to become one. Because of the spiritual significance of marriage, and because of its relationship to Christ and His Church, we need to look more closely at forgiveness.

Jesus, in dealing with the woman caught in adultery (see Jn. 8:3-11), does not give us a clear-cut answer to the question, "Should I continue in this relationship or not?" Adultery is sexual intercourse between two people of whom at least one is married. Was the woman brought before Jesus married, or

1.   *World Book Dictionary,* p. 838.

was the person with whom she was found? We might also ask, "Why didn't they bring the man who was involved in this sin?"

Another instance we should consider is the woman at the well (see Jn. 4:1-26). She had five husbands and the man with whom she was living at that time was not her husband. Again Jesus did not address the issue of whether she should have left the man. I believe Jesus dealt with this in Matthew 19:4-6.

And He answered and said unto them, Have ye not read, that He which made them at the beginning made them male and female, and said, For this cause shall a man leave father and mother, and shall cleave to his wife: and they twain shall be one flesh? Wherefore they are no more twain, but one flesh. What therefore God hath joined together, let not man put asunder (Matthew 19:4-6).

There is a point where we must set aside our emotions and what we would like to believe. This point is in how to deal with the statement, "What therefore God hath joined together, let *not* man put asunder [cut into pieces or into separate parts]." From my perspective, Jesus is saying that in God's original plan, a husband and a wife whom He puts together must stay together. No man or woman should attempt to pull apart what God has cemented as one flesh. When Jesus finished this statement, the Jews

Forgiveness: The Key to Divine Release

decided that He did not know the Scriptures. They said to Him, "How come Moses [think about this— they said *Moses*, not *God*] gave a command to give a bill of divorcement and to put her away?" Jesus floored them with His response:

> *He saith unto them, Moses because of the hardness of your hearts suffered you to put away your wives: but from the beginning it was not so. And I say unto you, Whosoever shall put away his wife, except it be for fornication, and shall marry another, committeth adultery: and whoso marrieth her which is put away doth commit adultery* (Matthew 19:8-9).

Is Jesus saying that adultery is the only grounds for putting away a spouse when it involves two Christians, or should we take the whole statement in verses 8 and 9 as one? If we take it as one, there is room for restitution, for restoring the relationship to its original state, even when adultery is involved.

Not too long ago there was a knock on my door. I opened the door slowly and when I looked to see who it was, I saw a familiar face. She had attended services many times in the past, sometimes regularly, at other times sporadically, but always with a smile. On this day, her smile lasted as long as it took her to close the door behind her. Suddenly her whole countenance changed. Before I could inquire about the reason for her sad look, tears were streaming down

Wives, Forgive Your Husbands

her face and dropping onto the floor. I invited her to sit, offered her a tissue, and waited for her to compose herself and tell me what had happened.

It took her some time, but finally she looked at me and said, "Pastor, you would not believe this," and with those words she looked up to the ceiling and down again as the tears flowed more intensely into the tissue. I knew whatever the problem was, it had to be very serious.

I gave her some more tissues and said, "Tell me what has happened." She looked up once more, then straight at me, and said, "Pastor, my husband is gay." It was a chilling experience for me. It is one thing when you hear news about people you don't know too well, but when it is someone you know, it is more personal. Momentarily I was struck speechless; then I sought a word of wisdom from the Holy Spirit. Many times I have heard the statement, "Silence is golden." It was so true at that moment. There have been certain occasions where I could give an immediate answer to someone's question. This time I realized that if I said the wrong thing, I could cause her to walk away, never to return. Or worse, her mind could snap and she could lose her reasoning. I held my tongue while I prayed for God's unction.

She looked directly at me and I knew I had to communicate by words and actions that I shared her hurt and disappointment. After a few moments, I

Forgiveness: The Key to Divine Release

broke the silence and asked how she knew her husband was gay. Without hesitation she outlined a series of circumstances that left no room for doubt that what she said was the truth. We prayed for strength and the Lord's wisdom to walk through—what was to her—the most difficult experience of her life.

Until the middle to late 1980's, I believe most people generally never envisioned such situations as being a part of their lives. Now it seems that no one knows what will happen next. The enemy is working in every conceivable way to destroy those whom God has joined together. It is up to the child of God to decide which way the pendulum will swing—toward God's plan or the devil's. The Bible states that the devil has come to steal, to kill, and to destroy (see Jn. 10:10). This lady realized that God's will is the best way for her, so she believed God to help her forgive her husband and restore her marriage.

Jesus said that the hardness of the people's hearts caused Moses to give them a bill of divorce, and that the original plan was still in place. Wife, do not harden your heart against your husband. I know it is hard when your husband betrays you. One person said to me, "Pastor, if he hid it when he ran around, it would not have been so hard for me. But he does it in the open and everybody sees him. Should I forgive him if he repents?" Jesus answers that question this way: "If it is the sin of adultery

Wives, Forgive Your Husbands

and you want to be hard-hearted, then divorce him [this is the only sin that falls in this category]." But if your desire is to follow God's plan, then He calls for forgiveness and the restitution of the marriage. Remember, Jesus paid the ultimate price to put us back under the original plan.

Let me close this chapter with the testimony of one Christian woman who loved God enough to seek Him for the restitution of her family. The purpose of this testimony is to let all flesh know that Jehovah God is Lord of all, and that there is still power in the blood of His Son, Jesus Christ—power to restore and power to set men free from the clutches of darkness. It is my prayer that this testimony will be a blessing to others. *To God be the glory!*

Testimony of Sister Archer

"As a child growing up, I was always curious about life and situations. If I saw a crowd gathered, I would always want to investigate the reason for the crowd. My mother, who was not a Christian at the time, did not believe this was a very good practice for her daughter. I remember her saying to me over and over, 'You are too nosey. You will bring disgrace upon the family.' Time and time again those negative words were spoken to me.

"After a while those words got into my spirit, to the extent that I thought of myself as a nobody. I became very self-conscious and developed a tremendous inferiority complex. My friends thought I had it all together, but many times I was hiding my hurts and feelings of insecurity. At night I would abandon the facade and cry myself to sleep, feeling sorry for myself and asking, 'Why was I born? Why can't I be happy like others?'

"This feeling of inadequacy spilled over into my adult life and, ultimately, into my married life. Even though my husband told me over and over that he loved me and showed me his love in many ways, I did not believe I was worthy of his love. It seemed as if I was constantly asking him, 'Do you love me?' or 'Do you still love me?' Sometimes my husband would say to me, 'I do not know why you are so unsure of yourself. What is wrong?'

"I was at that point in my life where I felt that peace, joy, and fulfillment were not meant for me. All I could see in my future were pain and sorrow. I did not like the torment I was putting myself through and I tried to be different and change myself, but I failed over and over again.

"In the meantime, my marriage started to fall apart. Eventually my husband and I separated. I was filled with bitterness and resentment toward my husband and my mother because I felt they had messed up my life. I was also very angry at my husband for his inconsistency with the support payments for our children. It angered me that he always

Wives, Forgive Your Husbands

seemed too busy with his girlfriends to spend quality time with his children. I was a very angry woman!

"There is a lot more I could say about the negative side of my old life, but the purpose of this testimony is to tell of God's amazing grace.

"In 1982 I started attending God's Battalion of Prayer Church. I was moved to tears as I heard them sing 'I will serve thee because I love thee.' The song goes on to say, 'Heartaches, broken pieces, ruined lives are why Christ died, Your touch is all I long for, You have given life to me.' Oh! How I needed to experience God's touch in my life—a life that seemed to be going nowhere. I was all dressed up at that service, looking good on the outside, but feeling very empty on the inside.

"Then I remembered that I had given my heart to the Lord in high school, but I'd backslid shortly after graduation. During the service, I rededicated my life to the Lord, asking Him to live His life in me and through me. I also asked Him to cleanse me of all unrighteousness. A peace and a joy came over me and my heart just melted before the Lord.

"At that time I was seeing a gentleman and the Lord delivered me from that relationship, which was contrary to His will for my life. As I continued attending God's house and hearing the Word of God, step by step I was able to overcome my fears, hurts, resentment, bitterness, and anger against others.

Forgiveness: The Key to Divine Release

God responded by giving me His peace that passes all understanding, His love, and His joy. Everything that I needed in this life I found in Him, so I stopped blaming others and instead started claiming His abundant life.

"One day the Lord told me to ask my mother's forgiveness for my years of resentment toward her. I did so and my mother started to weep. Then we were both crying. Mother asked me to forgive her because she did not know that her words had affected me that way. I told her that I had already done so and that I had baptized myself with God's sayings rather than man's sayings. Praise God! God then caused my mother and I to have a beautiful mother/daughter relationship until the day she was called home to glory.

"Eventually the Lord started telling me that He was going to restore my marriage. Even though I had forgiven my husband for his lack of commitment to our children, I had no desire at that time to be reconciled to him. To be perfectly honest, I resisted God on this matter and I tried to show Him why it should not be so and why it would not work. God was very patient with me, and every issue I brought up, God addressed. Eventually I found myself wanting the same things God wanted for me and my family. I discovered that I had so much love to give to my husband. I also discovered that I was no longer that old insecure wife, but a new wife who could do all things through Christ who strengthens me.

"The Lord started to give me a strategy—when to call him, what to say to him, and how to loose him from a long relationship. As my light continued to shine before my husband, I could sense the Lord drawing him and I started cooperating with the Lord more and more, for at that point I wanted my husband back. I wanted our marriage to be restored because the Lord had decided to restore it and I felt so blessed and honored that God Almighty, my Lord, was on my side.

"This is the same God who saved me and dried up my tears, took away my fears, and who healed my daughter of a disease the doctors said was incurable. Why should I resist such a God, who is all-wise, all-knowing, and all-powerful?

"To make a long story short, on August 16, 1993, after being separated from my husband for 16 years, the Lord caused my children and me to board a plane from New York to Moreno Valley, California, to take up residence with my husband. As I write this testimony in my new home, I give God all the praise, honor, and glory because nothing is impossible with Him and He is not finished with us. Amen."

Chapter 6

Husbands, Forgive Your Wives

The question is often asked, "Why do men get away with so many things, yet when a woman does the same she is severely criticized and often shunned?" This is a valid question. Preferential treatment for the husband seems to be a universal fact.

In Chapter 5 we considered Matthew 19:4-6. In another aspect of this passage, this discussion, which led Jesus to remind the Pharisees of God's original plan, deals with the way a man goes about the process of divorce. The discussion seems to favor men, since women are not mentioned. Notice the way the Pharisees fail to mention or express any consideration for forgiveness or restoration.

Forgiveness: The Key to Divine Release

Husbands are not exempt from the biblical commands to forgive. In the same way God has forgiven man, he is to forgive others—particularly his wife. After all, she is his own flesh, bone of his bone. If he cannot forgive his wife, how can he expect his heavenly Father to forgive him?

Jesus is never sidetracked by man-made traditions. He always keeps His eye on the Source. Every decision He makes and every word He speaks are based on His Father's will and plan. At the beginning, God created one man and one woman to be together forever. They were to find fulfillment in each other. God decided the ideal person for Adam was Eve, so He created her to be a suitable help.

Marriages are usually the outcome of a man's deep love for a woman to whom he is attracted and with whom he feels he can share his life. Too often, though, the relationship sours and ends in divorce. Once divorced, each partner may slide from one disastrous relationship to another, a situation that could have been averted if forgiveness had been practiced.

In Matthew 19:3, the Pharisees start the whole issue by asking, "Is it lawful for a man to put away his wife for every cause?" In other words, can a man divorce his wife for any frivolous reason? (Again, they don't ask, "Does he need to forgive her?") This is the question that caused Jesus to remind the people of God's original plan.

Go with me for a moment to the beginning and let's imagine what might have taken place. Imagine that the council of Jehovah (the Father, the Son, and the Holy Spirit) was considering the process of creation. They decide to create someone like Themselves. They will pour Their Spirit in him and through him; They will create an eternal kingdom on earth as it is in Heaven. Before man is created, though, it is necessary to create a suitable environment for him. So God creates the earth and places everything that man will ever need at his disposal.

God shapes man from the earth, breathes the breath of life into him, and man becomes a living soul to live forever with God. After God makes every provision for man, including a wife, man disobeys God. Adam does exactly what God told him not to do. "Do not eat of the fruit of the tree of knowledge of good and evil, for in the day you eat you will die" (see Gen. 2:17). The command against eating of this tree is to keep man from destruction and to bring glory to the triune God. The Bible says that God enjoyed coming down in the cool of the day to fellowship with His creation. This is the dividend that God received for His investment.

Just as God is reaping the fruits of His investment, man blows the whole thing. The woman, being

Forgiveness: The Key to Divine Release

the weaker vessel, is deceived by the devil and disobeys the command of the Lord. God's punishment is swift. The Bible describes the incident in this way:

Now the serpent was more subtil than any beast of the field which the Lord God had made. And he said unto the woman, Yea, hath God said, Ye shall not eat of every tree of the garden? And the woman said unto the serpent, We may eat of the fruit of the trees of the garden: but of the fruit of the tree which is in the midst of the garden, God hath said, Ye shall not eat of it, neither shall ye touch it, lest ye die. And the serpent said unto the woman, Ye shall not surely die: for God doth know that in the day ye eat thereof, then your eyes shall be opened, and ye shall be as gods, knowing good and evil. And when the woman saw that the tree was good for food, and that it was pleasant to the eyes, and a tree to be desired to make one wise, she took of the fruit thereof, and did eat, and gave also unto her husband with her; and he did eat (Genesis 3:1-6).

The last phrase in this Scripture is the reason men must forgive their wives. Let us face it, men. God says that the wife is the weaker vessel. That last phrase in Genesis 3:6 states that she, the weaker vessel, gave the fruit to her husband and he ate. At the moment she offered him the fruit, he held the key to obedience. He could unlock the door, go in, and eat the fruit; or he could obey God and refuse to listen to his wife. If he were the husband he should

Husbands, Forgive Your Wives

have been, satan would not have had an opportunity to convince Eve to eat in the first place. Throughout the whole dialogue, Adam is nowhere around. He should have been at Eve's side, ready to protect her from the devil's influence. Instead he let her bear the pressure alone.

After she succumbed to the devil's tempting, she went to her husband Adam. Unfortunately he did not tell her that she was wrong to disobey God's command. I believe that if Adam had stood his ground and resisted the devil, all who followed would have avoided the consequences of Adam's transgression. If he had not eaten the fruit, he would have remained sinless. He could have redeemed his wife and preserved a life in the presence of God for himself and for the human race.

Until the end of verse 6, the woman is battling with the devil alone. Then the man appears and joins her in the sin. The woman by herself cannot establish sin. The Bible says it takes two to establish a thing (see 2 Cor. 13:1), so the man appears and establishes sin. From that moment on, the behavior of the man was set. When we read verse 7, we see the effect of their decision.

And the eyes of them both were opened, and they knew that they were naked; and they sewed fig leaves together, and made themselves aprons. And they heard the voice of the Lord

Forgiveness: The Key to Divine Release

God walking in the garden in the cool of the day: and Adam and his wife hid themselves from the presence of the Lord God amongst the trees of the garden (Genesis 3:7-8).

It was God's pleasure to come and fellowship with them, but on this occasion we see an example of their joint behaviors. Adam and his wife "hid themselves from the presence of the Lord God amongst the trees of the garden."

The Lord stops looking and calls, "Adam, where art thou?" They are hiding together, but now God confronts the man. He is the person entrusted with the responsibility for his actions and those of his wife. He is charged to oversee and make sure everything is in order. Suddenly, the union comes to a screeching halt. Genesis 3:10-12 shows the end of their togetherness.

And Adam said, "I heard Thy voice in the garden, and I was afraid, because I was naked; and I hid myself." God replies, "Who told thee that thou wast naked? Hast thou eaten of the tree, whereof I commanded thee that thou shouldest not eat?" Here man's accountability is questioned. His response is, "The woman whom Thou gavest to be with me, she gave me of the tree, and I did eat." After blaming God and Eve for his sin, at least he admits that he ate. It is a clear case of self-righteousness.

Husbands, Forgive Your Wives

Self-righteousness is the reason a man finds it so difficult to forgive his wife when she sins against him. He fails to see how he has sinned against his heavenly Father and needs God's forgiveness. Remember, husband, you too have sinned against God and need His pardon. He has said if you cannot pardon your wife, He will not pardon you. I ask you, "Can you live without God's pardon?" Check with King David to find out what happens when you try to live outside of God's pardon.

Have mercy upon me, O God, according to Thy lovingkindness: according unto the multitude of Thy tender mercies blot out my transgressions (Psalm 51:1).

David knew it was important for his transgressions to be removed. In Psalm 51:8-9, he says that he has no joy, no gladness. His bones are broken and God has hidden His face from him. David makes it abundantly clear in this Psalm that everyone needs God's forgiveness. The surest way to receive it is to first forgive those who have sinned against us.

One Sunday morning following our 11:30 service, I moved to the door to thank everyone as they were leaving. A very distinguished member of the congregation came over to greet me. Her face was filled with a smile, much broader than usual. She introduced a friend she had invited to church. I greeted the man warmly as he told me how much he was

Forgiveness: The Key to Divine Release

blessed by the service. I told him that I hoped he would return often.

Before she moved away, this sister asked if she could see me as soon as I was through greeting everyone. I agreed and when I entered my office, she and her friend were waiting for me. I offered them a seat and asked the reason for their visit. She began to speak of the gentleman and I could see she was quite excited. She explained that he was a successful businessman and that he would like to become a member of the church. She continued to impress me with his credentials; then she told me that he was in love with her and she with him. In fact, they planned to marry and wanted to know if I would marry them.

Because I did not know the man, I began to ask him a few preliminary questions. I was surprised to learn that this pillar of a man was leaving his wife and seven children. He planned to marry this woman because his wife of many years did not do things to please him. I explained to him that he was sinning against God and his family and if he did not seek to be reconciled to his family, he would be called to account before God.

I believe it is the unwillingness of men to forgive their wives that has led to the mess marriages are in today. I know of a man who had to rely on others to help him finance his college education. After he graduated, he got a prestigious position in a large corporation. Suddenly, he considered his wife inferior to him. He began to hold her accountable for every mistake she made, so he could justify leaving her for someone else. He got his way eventually, but some time later he went to his former wife's mother and, on bended knee, admitted how foolish he had been.

When unforgiveness is allowed to develop, homes are broken apart. Usually the results of a broken home are worse than the original conditions. Some men cannot overlook or are not willing to forgive a wife who purchases things without his permission. Others hold it against the wife when she fails to approve of an expensive purchase, such as a new car, simply because she feels they cannot afford it.

Of course, there are some wives who provoke their husbands to the point where they break. These should emulate the wife of Proverbs 31, a wife the Bible calls a "virtuous woman"; her price is far more than rubies (verse 10). This woman will cause the heart of her husband to safely trust in her and she will do him good. She is described as industrious and is an entrepreneur. She makes wise investments and she "brings home the bacon."

There are also some wives who break up their own homes. Others spend unwisely. For such a woman, shopping seems to be a form of therapy. Their husbands can never earn enough to pay for their ego trips. He comes home every day to a dissatisfied wife. Still, a husband must forgive such a wife

Forgiveness: The Key to Divine Release

and pray for her deliverance. God is still able to do exceedingly abundantly above all that you can ask, think, or desire (see Eph. 3:20).

The most difficult case of all to forgive is the unfaithful wife. Every time I have to counsel a husband and wife where there is sexual unfaithfulness, it is a painful process. Thank God, I am not faced with this situation every week. As infrequent as such counselling is, it is still too often. Usually a couple comes to me to discuss problems in their marriage. After several sessions I discover there is an underlying problem and that what we are dealing with are only the symptoms. In these sessions, we spend a lot of time on symptoms before we get to the real problem. In very few cases does the wife willfully cheat on her husband. There may be compelling reasons for her frustration. I often find husbands who do not provide for their wives or who are never there for their wives, but it seldom leads to adultery.

When there is sexual infidelity, everyone involved suffers. The hurt is not easy to overcome. Not only has the trust been broken, but it is often very difficult to rebuild the trust. One young lady who was having problems with her husband came to me. At first I was getting nowhere, so finally I asked her if she had ever been unfaithful to her husband. She said she had. Next I asked if her husband knew about her affair. She said that he was aware of it. After she described the affair, I asked the reason for

Husbands, Forgive Your Wives

her behavior. Her reply was, "I thought I could make him jealous, so he would care more for me." She did not know that such behavior only makes matters worse. She realized her mistake after the act was already committed and now she must seek her husband's forgiveness.

True Love Restores Relationships

Let us go again for a walk in that first garden. When you find it hard to forgive your wife and it seems easier to start another relationship, remember how it was in the first garden. Adam, instead of managing the garden for God, sold himself to the devil. He betrayed the trust that the Lord God had placed in him. He committed spiritual adultery. Jehovah Elohim was pleased to come down in the cool of the day and commune with him. After man's sin, what was our heavenly Father's response to the object of His love? Did He destroy the object of His love and say, "Let Me start over and make another man. Maybe he will be different, perhaps he will be more committed to Me. Perhaps a second creation will not let Me down"?

God really loved the man He made. He trusted him enough to place His entire creation in his care. Now He must find a way to bring Adam back to his rightful place. This is true love in action. True love will find a way to restore every relationship through forgiveness. Adam and Eve hid from God, but the

Forgiveness: The Key to Divine Release

Lord still sought them. When He did not see them, He called for them. They were naked and too ashamed to come out of their hiding, but the Lord found a way.

What the Lord did in the first garden, He did for all who would follow. He offered a temporary reprieve until His Son could come to the second garden and restore the relationship between God and His creation. There was no other way for God to get back the object of His love. His Son had to make the sacrifice on the cross. As He hung there, despite all that He had suffered, He cried out, "Father, forgive them; for they know not what they do" (Lk. 23:34).

Husbands, love your wives as Christ loves the Church. He gave Himself for it. (See Ephesians 5:25.) If you will use God's love, you will find a way to forgive even when it is hard. Remember, it is not our will we need to follow, but the will of the Father.

I urge all husbands to take seriously the advice of Peter as he wrote in First Peter 3:7: "Likewise, ye husbands, dwell with them [your wives] according to knowledge, giving honour unto the wife, as unto the weaker vessel, and as being heirs together of the grace of life; that your prayers be not hindered."

Chapter 7

Parents, Children, and Forgiveness

Kids are people too and the relationship between parents and children is oftentimes stormy, escalating into bitter fights fostered by anger and hatred. Any deep-seated resentment is often seen when parents die and the will is read.

Children who were the "favorites" receive all, if not most, of an estate, while those who were rejected receive little or nothing. It is sad when parents leave this world with unforgiveness in their hearts. They must stand before the Lord of glory where they will realize the fruit of their hard hearts. As I have quoted so often in the preceding chapters, God will not forgive those who are themselves unwilling to forgive.

Forgiveness: The Key to Divine Release

Why do parents find it so difficult to forgive their own children? Maybe if we understood the dynamics surrounding the lives of our children, we would not be so hard on them. Perhaps if we took more time to walk a little in their shoes, we would not be so quick to judge their actions. First of all, consider their birth. Children do not ask to be born. They are here because God is a God of creation. Our willingness to fulfill His design and participate in the process of creation produces offspring and continues the cycle of life. Except in the case of rape, every parent makes a conscious decision to bring forth a child.

Preparing for Parenthood

The truth is, not everyone is prepared for parenthood. Often couples want a child before they are ready for the responsibility. Untimely births often generate frustration, anger, and hate that might not have occurred if the parents were spiritually, emotionally, physically, and financially prepared. Let's examine each of these qualities in more depth, to help us understand the need for greater maturity and perhaps alert potential parents to their immaturity.

Spiritually: Spiritual maturity is to obey God's provision of procreation, which means to wait until a person is married to have children. When God decided that each species would bring forth offspring after its kind, He established elaborate conditions

Parents, Children, and Forgiveness

surrounding the process. It is the violation of His principles that causes unnecessary burden upon mother and child. Scientists have carried out several tests that prove God's ways are necessary for the proper development of children. For example, they took a group of young monkeys and split them into two groups. One group was fed through a mechanical feeder without any contact or touch from the mother. The second group was fed by the mother. Those who were touched and given affection were better developed.

God's way is for a child to be born into a home where two parents are available to assist the child in the process of growth. These two people should be brought together by Him and, in His presence, joined in holy matrimony. Union without a God-ordained marriage, and birth without a committed, married couple, are formulas for disaster.

Emotionally: Emotionally, the child who is conceived outside of matrimony begins to feel the effects of an uncertain future from the moment of conception. As soon as the unwed mother becomes aware of her pregnancy, she experiences fear. This is true of women who are older as well as those who are younger.

Often I will miss members of my church. When I inquire about them, I am at first given various excuses. Finally, through a friend or relative, I discover

Forgiveness: The Key to Divine Release

the women are pregnant. I try to contact them or I send messages to encourage them to come to see me and, usually, they will come. When they come into my office, they look down and there are tears in their eyes. As a pastor it saddens me, for I know some of the fears they are experiencing. They are not sure if the father will give them support. They are afraid of having to go through the pregnancy alone. As they sit and share what is happening with them, the emotional turmoil inside is evident. Their fears extend beyond immediate concerns.

They don't know what the future holds or how they will make it through life with a child and no husband.

Your child needs the foundation of an emotionally balanced home, if he or she is to be emotionally stable. If your child is denied the affection, the love, and the confidence of a secure home, it is possible that your child will not function as he or she should.

Physically: Sadly today, children are having children. Obviously these young mothers are not physically ready for childbirth. This produces anger that can separate parent and child. Child-bearing is handled better by those who are physically mature. Just because a young person has reached puberty, doesn't mean he or she has the right to use his or her life-producing organs.

Parents, Children, and Forgiveness

A girl often reaches puberty at age 12 and a boy at 14. Most will agree that a young person of 12 or 14 is not physically prepared to be a parent. There are laws in the books that forbid a 14-year-old to work full-time. A 14-year-old is not allowed a driver's license, even though he might know how to drive. Some children learn to drive at 12, but they have to wait until they are 16 or 17 years old and physically capable of driving a car. Insurance companies charge a higher rate for drivers who are under 25 years of age. So those who are not physically mature can have a negative effect on every aspect of life and on parent/child relationships particularly. These negatives lead to anger and hate.

Financially: Financial security should be a prime concern when a couple is considering parenthood. Before a child is born, the child needs prenatal care. A person who is not financially prepared might not be able to afford prenatal care. This can be harmful to the child's birth and development. The parents, not realizing that the lack of necessary care in the early development of the child is now responsible for the child's behavior, assume the child is developing normally. When problems occur—those that are the result of improper care in early life—the parent simply assumes the child is rebellious. The child, on the other hand, would like to function in an acceptable manner, but does not have the capacity to do so at this stage of development. This causes more frustration

Forgiveness: The Key to Divine Release

for the child and, in the end, he or she stops trying to conform to the parents' instructions. Then the child begins to do as he or she pleases, antagonizing the parents and escalating the problem to the breaking point. Each side is disgusted with the other and, in more severe cases, end up hating each other. Had the couple been financially prepared, they could have afforded proper care during the birth process.

Let God Build the House

Some parents do not understand the real reason for bearing children. Instead of understanding God's way, they develop their own concept of children and parenting. It is when they try to live out this concept that they run into trouble. I believe Psalm 127 is a good source to look to in trying to understand God's way.

Unless the Lord builds the house, its builders labor in vain. Unless the Lord watches over the city, the watchman stand guard in vain. In vain you rise early and stay up late, toiling for food to eat—for He grants sleep to those He loves. Sons are a heritage from the Lord, children a reward from Him. Like arrows in the hands of a warrior are sons born in one's youth. Blessed is the man whose quiver is full of them. They will not be put to shame when they contend with their enemies in the gate (Psalm 127 NIV).

One of the greatest singers of all time, Nat King Cole, sang a song with the words, "A house is not a

Parents, Children, and Forgiveness

home if you are not there." It makes no difference if the house is made of marble and has all the conveniences in place, when the Person who means the most is not there. This should be true for everyone. You cannot build a successful family except the Lord builds it. With God, there is power to forgive your children for sins they have committed against you. Without His power you will have a dysfunctional family; the children will misbehave and confusion will reign.

God is the most important family member. Each one of us must recognize this fact and give Him the rightful place in our families' lives. He wants to participate in the process of building sound family values and He wants to keep the family structure intact. "Unless the Lord watches over the city, the watchmen stand guard in vain" (Ps. 127:1b NIV). In and of ourselves, we cannot forgive. It is hard to forgive, especially when we have worked hard and given of our best to establish our children and they go in the opposite direction.

Parenting should be a joy, but you must learn the secret of resting in Him to get the full benefit of His strength, which is the source of the joy you seek. Children are a heritage from the Lord and a reward from Him. It is God's nature to bless His creation. His desire is for you to fulfill His purpose. He wants you to be fruitful and to multiply.

Forgiveness: The Key to Divine Release

There is joy and satisfaction in a loving relationship, especially a marital relationship that brings forth new life. God did not intend for children to produce hate and division. He says, "Like arrows in the hands of a warrior are sons born in one's youth" (Ps. 127:4 NIV). Arrows are designed to attack an enemy, not to be the enemy. Your children are designed to be a help to you, to make you feel safe and to help you fulfill your dreams for their lives. When you love and forgive your children, when you nurture them in a good home environment, they will not be a shame to you.

When preparing for parenthood God's way, you can be assured of His grace on the children you bring forth and the home you seek to establish. If you heed the Word of God, you will train your children in the fear and admonition of the Lord. God always stands by His Word. He says, "Train up a child in the way he should go: and when he is old, he will not depart from it" (Prov. 22:6). The same verse in the New International Version reads, "Train a child in the way he should go, and when he is old he will not turn from it." It is clear that the proper application of God's Word will produce children who do not waver in their walk with the Lord.

Many parents question the efficacy of this verse when they see their children behaving contrary to everything they were taught. God does not lie; whatever He

Parents, Children, and Forgiveness

has said He will do. Parents need to understand the phrase "when he is old." This means when the child is older and in the Hebrew can mean "an aged" person. You may not live to see your child turn from the wrong way to the right way, but if God says He will do it, you can rest assured it will come to pass. Wouldn't it be a shame for you to leave this life with unforgiveness toward your child? Afterwards he turns to God, repents, and loves God with all of his heart. Who knows, he may even get into the ministry and lead thousands to Christ. If you remain unwilling to forgive him for the wrong things he did, none of what God uses him to do will be credited to your account.

Often a child is not consistently bad or does wrong things. He may be an obedient child, doing well at school, entering college, and continuing to get high grades. He may even be on the Dean's list. Everyone speaks well of him and you can see him accomplishing the things you were not able to do. You take off on an ego trip boasting to your relatives and friends how well your child is getting on with his studies. You expound on the profession he will soon be entering. Then, in the midst of your ego trip, your child is invited to go for a drive with a couple of his college buddies. One thing leads to another and before he knows it, these "buddies" rob a convenience store. What can he do? He is innocent, but who would believe him? As they speed from the scene of the crime,

Forgiveness: The Key to Divine Release

a state trooper appears in pursuit. Soon other police cars appear and block the road. With no place to turn, your son wishes the earth would open up and swallow him. He and his friends are arrested for armed robbery.

The phone rings as you are telling a friend of the great things your son is doing at college. The voice at the other end is faint and trembling. You hear your son say, "Mama, I am in trouble." Your first thought is that he failed a course or has had an accident, but as he explains, you wonder if what he is saying is true. You ask to speak to the police and they confirm your son is held along with two others for armed robbery. He tries to explain, but you are too hurt to listen. Too often it is not so much the trouble, but your pride that refuses to accept the truth and face the problem, that causes the hurt.

The point is, whatever your son or daughter has done, you are still required to forgive. Your daughter might have hurt you because she got pregnant or stole your money. Parents, remember that children are a gift from God, a heritage from Him. He only gives good things to His children, so why see your children as evil? Why do you find it hard to forgive them? It is because parents fail to understand that parenting is a partnership with God. He never expects them to handle these situations alone. God says that if each of us will acknowledge Him in all our ways, He will direct our paths (see Prov. 3:6).

Parents, Children, and Forgiveness

All through the Bible, we read of parents asking God to be an integral partner of their parenting experience. The first parents named their son Cain. His name means "a man received from the Lord." Joseph named his firstborn son Manasseh, "For God hath made me forget all my toil, and all my father's house." He named his second son Ephraim, "For God hath caused me to be fruitful in the land of my affliction" (Gen. 41:51-52.) Hannah also recognized that parenting is a partnership with God. She named her son Samuel, "Because I have asked him of the Lord" (1 Sam. 1:20).

Parents, if you find it hard to forgive and love your children, just pick up your phone or talk to couples who have been praying for years for God to bless them with a child. So many things are taken for granted. Like Hannah, everyone who is blessed with a child should do two things: (a) show your appreciation to God by truly giving that child back to God in solemn dedication; and (b) love your child enough to find room to forgive him if and when he messes up.

Hannah prayed for years for a child. Everybody knew she wanted a child, but they also knew she could not become pregnant. Finally, she got desperate.

And she was in bitterness of soul, and prayed unto the Lord, and wept sore. And she vowed a vow, and said, O Lord of hosts, if Thou wilt indeed look on the affliction of Thine handmaid, and remember me, and not forget Thine hand-maid, but wilt give unto Thine handmaid a man child, then I will give him unto the Lord all the days of his life, and there shall no razor come upon his head (1 Samuel 1:10-11).

She was in such bitterness of soul as she poured out her heart unto the Lord that the priest thought she was drunk. He said to her, "How long will you be intoxicated? Put away your wine from you" (see 1 Sam. 1:14). Then she answered, "No, my Lord, I am a woman of a sorrowful spirit: I have drunk neither wine nor strong drink, but have poured out my soul before the Lord. Count not thine handmaid for a daughter of Belial: for out of the abundance of my complaint and grief have I spoken hitherto" (1 Samuel 1:15-16).

Hannah knew that children were a heritage from the Lord. She did not take bearing children lightly. She knew that if God did not give children, people would be left empty and unfulfilled. Nothing could have taken the place of motherhood in Hannah's life. She also was not about to live with unforgiveness even before she got pregnant. She promised to give the child back to God if He would bless her with a boy. She wanted God to have equal rights to her son. If God would take away her reproach and give her the joy of motherhood, then she would, just as freely, give him back to the Lord.

Parents, Children, and Forgiveness

It is easier to forgive your child when your concept of him is correct. If you feel he is your personal possession, then you must always control your personal possession. But if you know your children are not your personal possession, then you will raise them to go and fulfill God's purpose for their lives. Your daily prayer will be: "Lord, they are yours. You gave them to me to train up for You. I have done my part and now they are Your responsibility."

I cannot imagine a parent seeing his children through the eyes of God and still finding it difficult to forgive them for what they do. Remember that before they hurt you, they hurt the Lord. If He can forgive them, why can't you? The fact that you cannot forgive clearly shows that you have a serious problem. You need to have a talk with the Lord and ask Him to take away your selfish pride, to see your children as He sees them, sinners for whom Christ died.

Too many children live with serious hurts because they never receive love and affection from their parents. Because they crossed their parents' paths the wrong way, they are rejected. Let me ask you this: "Are you willing for God to reject you, rather than open your heart and forgive your children?" I sincerely hope this is not the attitude of any of us. Jesus came to remove our hearts of stone and give us hearts of flesh, hearts that are tender toward our children.

Chapter 8

Forgiving Family Members

Fathers and Stepfathers

Time after time I am asked this question: "Pastor, do I have to forgive my father since he was never there for me?" Or I am told, "You should have seen how my father treated us when we were small. He treated my mother as if she was less than a servant. He never gave her money or provided for us. My mother had to go out and work hard to raise us. Pastor, I can't forgive my father. You did not grow up the way I did so you can't understand. I can't forgive him."

So many fathers alienate themselves from their families and then find themselves in bondage both to their families and to God. Too many men have failed

Forgiveness: The Key to Divine Release

to fulfill their role as father to their children or step-children. Fathers are designed by God to represent Him on the earth. As He is your Father in Heaven, so you, father, are to demonstrate what He is like to your children here on the earth.

For one thing, children do not come with an instruction manual. When I buy a car or an appliance, I expect to get an instruction manual. This manual tells me how the manufacturer expects the product to work and provides instructions for getting the maximum service from the product. The manual God provides for people is the Bible. It records how the process of fatherhood started. The reason for man's depravity, and the reason so many people are hurting, is because of man's failure to uphold the divine principles of fatherhood.

When God formed man in His own image, He designed him to be a representative figure. Man was to follow God's ways, carry out God's commands, demonstrate God's attributes, exercise God's manners, and develop godly character in his life.

After God provided for man's every need, He began to teach him responsibility. Man had to take care of his surroundings. In providing man with a help-meet, He set the stage for marriage and parenthood. God told Adam and Eve to be fruitful, fill the earth, and develop the human race after the pattern He had taught them. Another part of our responsibility

Forgiving Family Members

before God is to acknowledge that all have sinned and done evil. Once we understand our shortcomings, which are common to all of mankind, then we must be willing to forgive each other. A father who has failed to fulfill his God-given role has sinned, not only against his family, but also against God.

In Psalm 11:3 the question is asked, "If the foundations be destroyed, what can the righteous do?" Today, more than ever, the foundation of the home and family is being destroyed. Therefore, it is necessary that the family be structured on solid, godly values and principles. A man who desires to start a family must know God and must be a disciple of righteousness. He must be a good provider so he will be free to initiate and uphold sound moral values in his household. A good father will raise his children in the ways of God and prevent the erosion of the foundation of the family structure that is so prevalent in today's society.

Sin reduces man's ability to do what is good. Before man sinned, he had direct fellowship with God in a perfect environment. However, the day he sinned, his eyes were opened to evil and his fellowship with God was broken. Adam did not need God to tell him that he sinned; his own eyes had been opened. He saw his nakedness and tried to cover himself by sewing fig leaves. It was a futile attempt to hide from God.

Forgiveness: The Key to Divine Release

God had warned Adam that the day he ate the fruit of that tree, he would die. Adam and Eve deserved to die, but we see the reaction of a loving Father toward His earthly children. God did not respond to Adam in the way he deserved. Adam knew that he was no longer worthy to stand in the presence of God, so he hid himself. But God so loved His children that He made the first move to reconcile His relationship with sinful man. He did not wait for Adam to go to Him, even though Adam had sinned hopelessly when he deliberately disobeyed God's command. It was God the Father who sought him out and began the process of reconciliation. The Father began by confronting him with his sin and showing him the gravity of his actions. By admitting his error, Adam opened the way for the Father to forgive him. This produced the basis upon which the relationship could utimately be restored through Jesus Christ.

If we expect our heavenly Father to forgive us our sins, then we must be willing to overlook and forgive the numerous lapses and shortcomings of our own fathers, regardless of how difficult such a task may seem.

What are some of the things of which fathers are guilty? At the head of the list is cruelty to their family by physical abuse. I listened to one young man who said, "I do not know how to forgive my father because he was such a cruel man." I asked him if his father drank. He replied that as far as he knew, his

Forgiving Family Members

father never drank any alcohol. He was just a cruel man. The young man said, "My mother could never please him no matter how much she tried. For us children, it seemed as though his greatest pleasure was to beat us up. I was afraid of my father. The happiest times were with our mother when he was not at home. As soon as we saw him coming, we became like scared rats looking for a hole in which to hide. Over the years, I grew to hate him and I could not wait to be old enough to start working so I could leave the home. Man! the happiest day for me was when I left home. I was free of him at last!"

I asked him if he visited his parents' home now. "Yes," he said, "but only because of my mother. Were it not for her, I would not even go there." I asked, "Did you say anything to your father when you went home or if you saw him on the street?" He replied, "Well, if I go home and he is there I say 'Hello,' but that is it." "And what about when you see him on the street?" I asked. "Man, if I do not have to see him, that is fine with me," he replied. "This guy was like a beast. You would not imagine some of the cruel things he did to me. I do not like to talk about growing up. It made me so angry when I remembered the things I went through and how defenseless my mother was to come to my rescue. How do you expect me to forgive such a man?"

Someone else told me, "When my father was not drinking he was the nicest person around, but as

Forgiveness: The Key to Divine Release

soon as he started drinking with his friends, his entire personality changed. He would come home and nag at my mother until she answered him and then a fight would ensue. Sometimes, if our friends were visiting us when he came in drunk, he would insult them and embarrass us in their presence." "Was he a good provider?" I asked. "If he had money and he wasn't out drinking, he would give money to my mother. Many times we had to go without, but not because he did not work for a good salary. He made good money; he was just mean when he drank. Often, most of his earnings were gone when he came home after a drinking spree, and we had to make do with what was left.

"I would have been satisfied if I knew my father couldn't do any better, if he was uneducated and had to take a job that did not pay a large salary. I could understand that we had to make out with less. But it hurts to know that my father had the ability to take good care of his family and did not. I had to go out and deliver newspapers and do odd jobs to help finance the home and stay in school. I could not even get financial aid because of his income. I had to take out loans and now I have all these bills to pay. Meanwhile, he continues to spend all his money uselessly on alcohol. I must forgive him? No, I don't think so, not for what I went through. When I needed him most he was too busy having a good time. You can't be serious about wanting me to forgive him."

Forgiving Family Members

A young person came to me one day seeking my advice on a way to pray more effectively. She said, "Every time I go to pray there is a blockage. I can't seem to pray." The Holy Spirit directed me to ask about her childhood. "Were you happy at home with your father and mother during your childhood days?" The young lady immediately looked up to the ceiling of my office and said, "I do not want to get into that. Can you just tell me how to pray, how to overcome these blockages when I go to pray?" I told her, "One cannot separate one's self from one's past. If as a Christian, there is something in your past which you have not confronted, it will continue to be a hindrance to you no matter what you try to do." She paused for a moment and said, "All right, if I have to, then I will." She went on to say that her life was pleasant at home with her parents until her mother left for the United States to seek a better life for her family.

Shortly after her mother's departure, her father began seeing someone else and left the children alone at home for days, sometimes without anything to eat. He did not seem to care. The situation got so bad that one of her aunts took her to live with her. She was glad to go because she thought her aunt really was concerned about her and wanted to help. It was not long before she realized all her aunt wanted was a servant to do all her work. She was not really interested in her niece's welfare. The girl's hurt was

Forgiveness: The Key to Divine Release

severe. It was spawned by her father's infidelity and fueled by her aunt.

Sadly, she stated, "While my father was having a good time with his lady friend, I knew my mother was trying to help make a better life for us. But my father was just selfish and did not care about his own family. He was the one who encouraged my mother to leave and then he forsook us and left us to suffer. Over the years I lost all respect for him. I do not care if he lives or dies. I have no feelings for him." With tears pouring down her cheeks, she said, "I can't forgive him. I will never forgive him."

It was clear that the cause of the hindrance in her prayer life was her unforgiving heart. She was hurting and had carried that hurt all these years. I said, "I know this must be very hard for you to have suffered so much when there was no need for it. Your father was there, but did not care. Yes, you have a right to be angry and upset, but do you realize that until you are prepared to deal with your past life, you will not be able to move forward in your relationship with God?" Her eyes lit up. Staring straight into my eyes, she asked if that was true. I replied, "Yes, you have to forgive your father. You are holding yourself in bondage if you do not forgive him. You must face him if you are to face yourself and move forward in God."

So many people are hurting in the world today because of fathers who have not fulfilled their

Forgiving Family Members

God-given responsibility. Some have failed in their commission and others by omission.

Another young man told me this story. His father and mother were married, but while he was still an infant she died, leaving his father to raise his children alone. The task became very difficult for him and sometime later he remarried, thinking that he would be able to give his children a better home. What he did not realize was the person he married did not know how to love and care for children. Maybe she did know, but was unable to control her temper. Eventually, the children became the victims of her uncontrolled anger. She treated them cruelly in the father's absence. The father always believed the reports she made against the children. Even though she had already spanked the children, the father spanked them a second time. This young man confessed that his childhood days were filled with hurt. He could not understand why his father never asked him or his brother or sister for their side of the story. He always believed his wife and punished them accordingly.

He said that as he got older, he began to hate his father because he thought his father did not care about them. "I thought of running away many times," he said, "but I had nowhere to run. I always told myself that one day, I would be old enough to work and take care of myself and that would be the last day my father would see me.

Forgiveness: The Key to Divine Release

"I endured until I was in my early teens and went to stay with a friend." "How old was your friend?" I asked. "Oh! he was about three years older than I," he replied. "Was he living by himself?" I asked. His answer was, "No, he was living with his parents, but he told his mother my situation and she asked his father for me to stay for a few days. I did not know what her plan was, but after a while, she arranged to see my father by himself. She took me to meet him and requested that he listen to what I had to say. I began to explain that most of the things we were being accused of were not true and I related all the things that were done to us in his absence." He said his father began to cry. The father explained to his son that his decision to get married was to provide a better home for his children. He never knew that instead of making it better he had actually made it worse for them.

This young man went on to say that from that moment he looked at his father differently. He knew then that his father really loved them, but had found himself between a rock and a hard place. His confrontation with his father made it easier for him to forgive.

Stories of certain stepfathers' treatment of children are too numerous to mention. I hear them so often that I wonder why mothers keep believing things will change for their children. Men make all

Forgiving Family Members

kinds of promises when they propose marriage. They promise to love their wife's offspring as their own. Then, after they are married, their love turns to hatred.

I was in my office one day when the phone rang. I picked it up and identified the church. A female voice came through, loud and clear: "May I speak to the pastor?" I replied, "Speaking." She began to tell me the sad story of the treatment her son received at the hands of his stepfather. She said her husband had promised her faithfully before they got married that he would love her son and treat him as his own, but from the time they got married the child did not have one happy day. With a tearful voice she said, "My son is 26 years old. He has lost his job and is finding it difficult to make his payments. He has asked my permission to use the basement of our house until he obtains another job and gets back on his feet. My husband will not agree even though we do not use the basement. He just hates my son. My son is so disappointed and I am angry. I am prepared to leave my husband this very minute."

Then there are stepfathers who make sure that their own children are well provided for, while their stepchildren are made to suffer unnecessarily, as slaves to their stepbrothers and stepsisters. I have counselled with women who were sexually molested by stepfathers. Each of the victims who has suffered

Forgiveness: The Key to Divine Release

at the hands of fathers or stepfathers asks the same question, "Do I have to forgive my father or stepfather?" I reply, "The Lord says, 'Yes, for if you forgive not your father or your stepfather, neither will I forgive you.' "

Remember, you cannot forgive these things by yourself. He who commands you to forgive will help you, if you truly desire to forgive.

Chapter 9

Forgiving Family Members

Forgiving Your Mother

From my experience as a pastor, I have found that most boys get along well with their mothers. As a matter of fact, I can clearly remember from my days at school that if you wanted to get into a fight with some boy, all you needed to do was make a negative statement about his mother. Then you better be prepared to defend yourself. Daughters are mostly the ones who carry hurts from their mothers, but I have also encountered a number of hurting sons too.

In a previous chapter we learned that man's problem started when he gained knowledge of evil. If man had known only good, this world would have been a beautiful place. Unfortunately, sin was introduced, and since then, all of us have sinned against

God and against each other. Some children find it hard to forgive their mothers because of the sin of adultery. Adultery occurs when a husband or wife has a sexual relationship outside of the marriage. Under Old Testament law, adulterers were stoned. This served as a deterrent to others who might be tempted to indulge in such sinful behavior.

God's original plan for the family was one in which the procreation of children was the outcome of a blessed and sacred marriage between a man and a woman. This relationship was the foundation on which the family unit was to be built. When this foundation was not in place, disintegration of the family structure with its accompanying problems would result. When God created the human race, His plan was for every man to have his own wife, every woman her own husband, and every child would have the comfort of a home with a mother and a father. This was a good plan, but our subversion of it to accommodate our desire to indulge in sexual relationships—in and out of wedlock—eroded the foundation.

When a man and woman are not married, the man has no commitment to her. He does not feel a bond with her. In most cases, he sees her as a convenience to satisfy his needs and desires. When he is satisfied, he treats her with indifference or he moves on to the next station. This is not according to God's

Forgiving Family Members

plan. God did not create women to be used by men. Unfortunately, this is often the result of sexual relationships before marriage.

Another negative effect of adultery is what happens to the children who are conceived outside of the comfort and confidence of marriage bonds. When an unmarried woman discovers that she is pregnant, it is often a traumatic experience for her. Her first impulse is fear. She is afraid that the biological father may not assume responsibility for fatherhood, and she feels the pressure to provide for the child by herself. She is afraid to face the world with confidence, and the guilt of sinning before God haunts her. Some of this fear may be transferred to the fetus and the child is scarred from birth. It is deprived of the security of a stable home environment where the father and mother are the primary care providers.

The dilemma and pain of the mother are further exacerbated by her inability to cope with the financial and emotional commitments of motherhood. The mother is angry with the child's father because he has abandoned her and her child. Sometimes the anger is transferred to the child, who may then be subjected to both physical and emotional abuse.

Sometimes the child is not adequately provided for since the mother may have to quit her job because of the pregnancy. Often her present job does not pay enough to take care of the child's needs. All these problems can have a severe impact on the social and moral development of the child. The child may lack the basic training in courtesy, honesty, and respect for authority. The child may not be aware of the existence of God because no parent is available to instruct the child in the ways of righteousness. A child, growing up in such an environment, may easily become a delinquent. If that trend is not checked, it can develop into serious criminal activities.

I believe that the firstborn suffers the most emotional trauma. The second time around, the mother is less fearful or worried about what people will say or think. The mother rationalizes, saying, "This is not the first time, so what's the big deal?" Little does the mother realize that the problem is not only fear, but also guilt and the disappointment of her immediate family. She is also a prime suspect to become enemy number one to her children as they grow older without a father. The suffering is not hers alone; the children must bear the consequences as well because they are the product of such a relationship.

When flying from New York to Antigua one day, I was assigned a seat in the airplane next to a beautiful young lady. Her destination was one of the smaller Caribbean islands. I noticed one of her legs was in a cast. She was friendly and a lively conversation developed between us. I learned she had suffered a broken leg when she jumped out of the

Forgiving Family Members

window of her home to escape being whipped by her mother. She had no reservations about discussing other personal matters with a stranger and by the time we parted, I had learned a great deal about her family.

She was one of four children and the only girl. Each of her siblings was fathered by a different man. Even though her mother was now a Christian and took her daughter to church with her regularly, her daughter's lack of respect for her mother was obvious. Her mother would not allow her to go out with her friends and that made the daughter very angry. She felt that a mother whose past was so checkered had no right to dictate how her daughter must live her life. The rift between them was so wide that she refused to live with her mother in the United States. She was returning to the Caribbean to live with her grandparents. She was comfortable with them and considered them appropriate role models.

For a child to leave her home, her mother, her brothers, her friends, and her school to start life anew in another country suggests that her hurt must be severe. She was going to continue her schooling in the Caribbean and return to the United States to pursue a college education, but she would not live with her mother. I must admit that this child had a determination to succeed. She had her life all planned out, but without her mother as part of it.

Forgiveness: The Key to Divine Release

Why did she hate her mother so? What went wrong in their lives that created such irreparable damage?

She told me her grandparents were not Christians. Were they responsible for their daughter's decision and change in life style? Would their daughter have become a better mother if she had been raised in a home where Christian principles were adhered to and moral values established? These were questions for which I had no answers. I did advise the young woman, however, to look to God for help. God loved her and would see her through any difficult moment if only she would ask Him to enter into her heart.

This girl's experience is by no means unique. Children all around us are embittered by incidents in their lives that they attribute to lapses on their mothers' part. Sometimes the hurt runs so deep they swear they can never forgive their mothers for the suffering they have caused them. Many factors may have contributed to the behavior of such mothers. Their own mother might have abandoned them at birth, not because she did not love them or care for them, but because she was afraid. Their father was not there to hold their hand and give them the assurance that everything was going to be all right.

Maybe, by having children out of wedlock, their mother was despised by her family and friends. She had to struggle alone to raise her children and the

Forgiving Family Members

strain was more than she could bear. Thus, the children became victims of her frustration. Sometimes there were moments in their lives when they wished they had died as a baby. They entertained negative thoughts during those times when their spirits were down and the world seemed to be crumbling around them. But our Lord God has promised He will never leave us nor forsake us (see Heb. 13:5). God has a plan for each of us. It is not right for us to pass judgment on our mothers; we do not know how we might have behaved under similar circumstances. Let us try to learn from our mothers' mistakes, and by God's grace, live a life that will bring praise, honor, and glory to His name.

Sin separates us from our heavenly Father. So you will never realize His plan for your life until you can confront whatever your mother has done and by the grace of God, say to her, "Mother, despite the past, you are my mother. God has given me to you and you to me. We have both failed Him, but He still loves us and is willing to forgive us as we forgive each other. Mother, from the depth of my heart, I love you and forgive you."

Remember, if you do not forgive your mother of her sins, neither will your heavenly Father forgive you of your sins. Forgiveness brings healing and God's outpouring of love and grace.

Chapter 10

Forgiving Family Members

Forgiving Brothers and Sisters

Therefore if thou bring thy gift to the altar, and there rememberest that thy brother hath ought against thee; leave there thy gift before the altar, and go thy way; first be reconciled to thy brother, and then come and offer thy gift (Matthew 5:23-24).

And when ye stand praying, forgive, if ye have ought against any: that your Father also which is in heaven may forgive you your trespasses (Mark 11:25).

According to these two Scriptures, we have a responsibility to forgive regardless of our own position in the process. To put it simply, we must address the

Forgiveness: The Key to Divine Release

need for forgiveness whether we initiated the transgression or if the transgression was against us. It is a matter of dual responsibility. We must make sure there is a clear channel between us and our brothers and sisters. This applies to siblings, step-siblings, and brothers and sisters in the spirit.

Cain and Abel

There is a chorus I have sung quite often since childhood. The words of the chorus are: "Since Jesus came into my heart, Since Jesus came into my heart, Floods of joy o'er my soul like the sea billows roll, Since Jesus came into my heart." Whenever I think of the words of this song, I am reminded that all is not lost because of sin. When sin entered the world, everything became chaotic. From the time man was created, God intended only goodness and peace toward His creation. He blessed them with all they would ever need, gave them authority over the earth, and blessed them with two sons. Their parents taught them that they each had a responsibility to Jehovah Elohim.

And Adam knew Eve his wife; and she conceived, and bare Cain, and said, I have gotten a man from the Lord. And she again bare his brother Abel. And Abel was a keeper of sheep, but Cain was a tiller of the ground. And in process of time it came to pass, that Cain brought of the fruit of the ground an offering unto the Lord. And Abel, he also brought of the

Forgiving Family Members

firstlings of his flock and of the fat thereof. And the Lord had respect unto Abel and to his offering: but unto Cain and to his offering He had not respect. And Cain was very wroth, and his countenance fell. And the Lord said unto Cain, Why art thou wroth? and why is thy countenance fallen? If thou doest well, shalt thou not be accepted? and if thou doest not well, sin lieth at the door. And unto thee shall be his desire, and thou shalt rule over him. And Cain talked with Abel his brother: and it came to pass, when they were in the field, that Cain rose up against Abel his brother, and slew him (Genesis 4:1-8).

How could Cain kill his brother when his brother had done him no wrong? I assume the parents of these boys taught them properly and told them they were to love each other. They also must have taught them the need for and the value of work, since each chose a particular work ethic. Abel, the younger, chose to raise sheep; Cain, the older one, decided to be a farmer. Each career was important. Cain provided the fruit of the ground, while Abel provided the milk and butter. (We do not find meat being approved by God for consumption until after the flood of Noah's time.) If we assume Adam was a normal father, he surely complimented his sons for the great job they were doing in providing for the needs of the family.

I can say without hesitation that each boy knew what God required of him. When they appeared

Forgiveness: The Key to Divine Release

before God with their offering, their lives took a dramatic turn. Cain brought a sacrifice that was not acceptable to God. The Lord would not have been just in rejecting Cain's offering if Cain did not know what was required of him. Cain was typical of so many people today who like to come to God on their own terms.

Cain's offering, the fruit of the ground, was not bad; it simply was not what God required. He required a blood sacrifice, a lamb without spot or blemish—a type pointing to the Lamb of God, the Lord Jesus Christ. The fruit of the ground represented man's effort. The fruit came from the same earth that was cursed because of Adam's sin of disobedience. The offering of Abel represented obedience and an acceptable sacrifice; Cain's represented disobedience and an unacceptable offering.

And in process of time it came to pass, that Cain brought of the fruit of the ground an offering unto the Lord. And Abel, he also brought of the firstlings of his flock and of the fat thereof. And the Lord had respect unto Abel and to his offering: but unto Cain and to his offering He had not respect. And Cain was very wroth, and his countenance fell (Genesis 4:3-5).

Cain's anger should not have been directed at his brother. His brother was not the one responsible for God's rejecting his offering. Cain himself chose to offer God an unacceptable offering. Maybe he decided

Forgiving Family Members

God was not really particular about the type of offering he could bring; nevertheless, his disobedience was costly. God's acceptance of Abel's offering and His rejection of Cain's offering was clear; Cain knew he had lost favor with God. His brother's acceptance, on the other hand, brought forth God's favor. God's pleasure was so obvious, it caused Cain to get angry with Abel. His anger was so great that he murdered him. God knew that if Cain's anger was not dealt with, it would lead to his destruction, so He confronted Cain.

> *And the Lord said unto Cain, Why art thou wroth? and why is thy countenance fallen? If thou doest well, shalt thou not be accepted? and if thou doest not well, sin lieth at the door. And unto thee shall be his desire, and thou shalt rule over him* (Genesis 4:6-7).

God showed Cain that his anger was misdirected. Cain should have seen his error and assumed responsibility for his own mistake. God wanted Cain to repent of his actions, to turn his anger and negative feelings into a positive response. Cain refused to accept God's advice. So instead he allowed his feelings of envy, which led him to kill his brother, to dominate his life. Perhaps, at the time he killed Abel, he thought that if his brother were no longer on the earth, God would have to accept his sacrifice.

> *And Cain talked with Abel his brother: and it came to pass, when they were in the field, that*

Forgiveness: The Key to Divine Release

Cain rose up against Abel his brother, and slew him (Genesis 4:8).

Jacob and Esau

All of us are familiar with the story of Jacob and Esau. You may not realize, though, how the best intentions of parents can cause problems for their children. Although they were twins, Esau was the first to be born and, as such, was entitled to the blessing of the firstborn. Isaac, their father, loved Esau because he was a hunter and supplied their home with venison, a meat he truly loved. Jacob, on the other hand, was the favorite of his mother Rebekah. On one occasion, when Esau was returning from a long hunting trip, he was weak with hunger. Jacob had prepared some lentil soup and bread and Esau asked Jacob to feed him to satisfy his hunger. Jacob agreed, but only if Esau would sell him his birthright in exchange for the food. Esau agreed. (See Genesis 25:27-34.)

Some years later, Isaac grew old and his sight began to fail. He decided to set his house in order and, as was the custom, he wanted to bless his firstborn son and give him his inheritance. First, though, he asked Esau to go out and get him some venison one last time before he died. While Esau was gone, Rebekah devised a scheme to have Jacob receive the blessing instead of Esau. She cooked some goat meat seasoned to resemble venison, dressed Jacob in hairy skins, and tricked Isaac into blessing the second-born son.

Forgiving Family Members

And it came to pass, as soon as Isaac had made an end of blessing Jacob, and Jacob was yet scarce gone out from the presence of Isaac his father, that Esau his brother came in from his hunting. And he also had made savoury meat, and brought it unto his father, and said unto his father, Let my father arise, and eat of his son's venison, that thy soul may bless me. And Isaac his father said unto him, Who art thou? And he said, I am thy son, thy firstborn Esau. And Isaac trembled very exceedingly, and said: Who? where is he that hath taken venison, and brought it me, and I have eaten of all before thou camest, and have blessed him? yea, and he shall be blessed. And when Esau heard the words of his father, he cried with a great and exceeding bitter cry, and said unto his father, Bless me, even me also, O my father. And he said, Thy brother came with subtilty, and hath taken away thy blessing. And he said, Is not he rightly named Jacob? for he hath supplanted me these two times: he took away my birthright; and, behold, now he hath taken away my blessing. And he said, Hast thou not reserved a blessing for me? And Isaac answered and said unto Esau, Behold, I have made him thy lord, and all his brethren have I given to him for servants; and with corn and wine have I sustained him: and what shall I do now unto thee, my son? And Esau said unto his father, Hast thou but one blessing, my father? bless me, even me also, O my father. And Esau lifted up his voice, and wept. And Isaac his father answered and said unto him, Behold, thy dwelling shall be the fatness of the earth, and of the dew of heaven from above; by thy sword shalt thou live, and shalt serve thy brother; and it shall come to pass when thou shalt have the dominion, that thou shalt break his yoke from off thy neck. And Esau hated Jacob because of the blessing wherewith his father blessed him: and Esau said in his heart, The days of mourning for my father are at hand; then will I slay my brother Jacob (Genesis 27:30-41).

It appears that Esau's preoccupation with hunting cost him the blessing and the birthright. In the first instance, it was hunger from hunting that forced him to give up the right to his inheritance for a piece of bread and a bowl of lentils. Then a second hunting trip prior to the ceremonial blessing gave Rebekah the opportunity to trick Isaac, costing Esau again.

When Esau heard the words of his father, he cried with a great and exceedingly bitter cry, and begged his father to bless him also. He charged his brother with deceit and claimed that Jacob had stolen his rightful blessing.

I often come in contact with people who may have a brother or sister with whom they have no close

Forgiving Family Members

contact. Some do not even know if their brother or sister is alive or dead. Children do not know their first cousins because their parents hold grudges against their siblings. In some, if not the majority of cases, animosity between siblings is caused by the inconsistency or favoritism of parents toward their children. One is preferred over the other, as in the case of Jacob and Esau. Their parents are guilty of being partial toward one child at the expense of the others.

Isaac's favorite was Esau and Rebekah's was Jacob. They made sure that each of the boys knew where they stood. If, as parents, Isaac and Rebekah had taught their sons to love each other as brothers, they might have avoided the conflict that followed. Isaac, as the priest of the family, would have blessed both of his sons fairly. Instead, they failed as parents and created an atmosphere for bitterness to develop between the two brothers.

Esau hated Jacob because of the blessing his father gave him, so Esau judged his father and purposed to kill his brother. When Rebekah learned of Esau's plan, she told Jacob to flee to her brother Laban, who lived in Haran. She wanted Jacob out of the way until Esau's anger subsided.

Jacob's deception was the source of his brother's anger, but his decision to run compounded the problem. Instead of seeking his brother's forgiveness, he

Forgiveness: The Key to Divine Release

ran away knowing his brother harbored unforgiveness against him in his heart. Jacob felt secure and safe while he was out of his brother's presence. He didn't realize that the unforgiveness between them would return to haunt him.

While he was with his uncle Laban, he was tricked too. Laban substituted his older, less attractive daughter Leah for Rachel, the woman Jacob thought he was marrying. Imagine his horror and disappointment when, on the morning after his wedding, he realized that his uncle switched the women before the ceremony. His bride was not Rachel, whom he loved, but her elder sister Leah. Retribution had taken its toll on his life.

And it came to pass, that in the morning, behold, it was Leah: and he said to Laban, What is this thou hast done unto me? did not I serve with thee for Rachel? wherefore then hast thou beguiled me? (Genesis 29:25).

Jacob's life was filled with disappointments and deception until he acknowledged his sin against Esau, confessed it to God, and sought his brother's forgiveness. It was a long process that he tried desperately to avoid, but he could find no place of rest. God promised him His blessing when he returned to his home in Bethel and confronted his brother Esau.

Jacob began the long journey to reconcile himself with his brother. He sent messengers to meet his

Forgiving Family Members

brother to tell him of his coming. The messengers returned to tell Jacob that Esau was on the way to meet him with an army of 400 men. When Jacob heard of Esau's response, he feared for his life and started to devise a scheme to save at least a portion of his goods. He divided his family and goods into two groups, thinking that one could escape if the other was captured. This scheme is a good example of man trying to solve a problem without God's help. Fortunately, Jacob came to his senses and turned to God in prayer.

And Jacob said, O God of my father Abraham, and God of my father Isaac, the Lord which saidst unto me, Return unto thy country, and to thy kindred, and I will deal well with thee: I am not worthy of the least of all the mercies, and of all the truth, which Thou hast shewed unto Thy servant; for with my staff I passed over this Jordan; and now I am become two bands. Deliver me, I pray Thee, from the hand of my brother, from the hand of Esau: for I fear him, lest he will come and smite me, and the mother with the children. And Thou saidst, I will surely do thee good, and make thy seed as the sand of the sea, which cannot be numbered for multitude (Genesis 32:9-12).

In his prayer, Jacob reminded God of all His promises, but he forgot that he was the one responsible for Esau's hatred. Jacob forgot, but God did not. Jacob

Forgiveness: The Key to Divine Release

needed to be reconciled to his brother if he expected God to bless him. When he had finished his prayer, Jacob made one last attempt to appease Esau. He sent his servants ahead with a substantial gift of livestock. Jacob had no idea how his brother would respond, so he stayed behind on the opposite side of the river.

While he was alone, God brought him face to face with the truth. The first step toward reconciliation is to acknowledge one's sin. When Jacob was alone, a man wrestled with him until daybreak. Although the man could not defeat Jacob, he was able to injure him by disjointing his thigh bone. Jacob still held on until the man blessed him. When Jacob told the man his name, the man said that he would no longer be called Jacob the Usurper, but Israel, a prince with power with God and men. Jacob realized that he had not been wrestling a man, but had come face to face with God. He made a decision to change his ways and God changed his circumstances.

When the man left, Jacob looked up to see Esau coming toward him.

He bowed low seven times to his estranged brother, expecting the worse. His fears were for nought. Instead Esau ran to meet him, embraced him, and kissed him. Together they wept.

The Lord promises that, if our ways please Him, He will cause our enemies to be at peace with us (see

Forgiving Family Members

Prov. 16:7). Pleasing the Lord includes forgiving those who are willing to humble themselves as well as those who will not humble themselves. We must also be aware of the fact that Esau was not obedient either. He disobeyed his father and married outside the land. He did his own thing and married more than one wife. (See Genesis 26:34.) Although God was not pleased with Esau, He would not allow Jacob to get away with what he had done. He had to seek his brother's forgiveness.

None of us will inherit God's blessing if we are not willing to forgive our brothers or sisters for the wrongs they may have done to us. Similarly, if we have wronged them, then we need to humble ourselves and seek their forgiveness. It does not make any difference whether they are Christians or not. Jacob was chosen of God, but for God to hear and answer his prayer, he had to make it right with his brother.

You may be saying to yourself that your circumstances are different. Maybe you are the child who has taken care of your parents, with little or no help from your brothers and sisters. Maybe you are the one who has paid for the repairs to the house and taken care of the doctor's bills. You have been unselfish in your devotion to your parents, never considering what you might get back in return for your efforts. You consider it your duty to take care of

Forgiveness: The Key to Divine Release

them. Still, you never expected your brothers and sisters to fight you for your parents' possessions. After all, they never helped in any way. This situation is difficult to reconcile.

Another possibility is that your parents may leave a will to be opened only after their deaths. Imagine your disappointment when you realize that you, who have done the most for your parents, receive the least. Your anger against your siblings cannot be contained. In your heart of hearts you find it difficult to forgive, since you have been hurt. So the enmity between you goes on unchecked for years. God is saying to you to forgive, for if you do not forgive, neither will you find forgiveness at the mercy seat of God.

If Esau, who was not living to please God, could forgive his brother for all he had done to him, how can you, a Christian, fail to forgive your brothers and sisters? You are making void the grace of God that was bestowed upon you, and the Lord will not hold you guiltless. So forgive them, as God has called you to do.

Chapter 11

Forgiving Your Pastor

One day, as I was listening to Dr. Narramore's radio program, "Psychology for Living," I realized he was dealing with a subject that was close to home. He was discussing children with emotional behavioral problems, who are unable to cope with the responsibilities of life. He stressed that because parents do not know what is happening with their children, they often discipline them for actions they have no control over. He went on to list some of the symptoms of children who may have experienced brain damage at birth, a chemical imbalance, or dyslexia.

Immediately I began to wonder if one of my children was suffering from one of these disorders. My wife and I had been thinking he was just disobedient. As soon as I arrived at my office, I decided to call

Forgiveness: The Key to Divine Release

Rosemead School of Psychology to find out more about this subject. A very courteous gentleman answered and I told him that I had heard the radio program and was calling to express my concern for one of my children. I told him that, if necessary, I would fly my child out to the clinic for treatment.

I soon discovered there were clinics throughout the country, and the gentleman recommended a center close to us. I did not act on the information right away. I considered the possibility that I had over-reacted to Dr. Narramore's program. Still, I could not get the thought out of my mind. When I finally decided to act on the information, I couldn't find the address, so I called the gentleman back. It was during this second call that he introduced me to the course for ministers and missionaries and suggested I take it.

I requested the package and in a few days it arrived. I examined the material and thought it would be good to attend. There was only one problem. The course began on February 9 and continued for two weeks. During that period our church sponsors an annual Valentine's Retreat, which my wife coordinates. I wrestled with the urge to go and after some deliberation, told her about the course. She said, "You cannot go. There is the Valentine's Retreat for the couples and I cannot do it by myself."

That settled the issue, or so I thought. I began to feel uneasy about not taking the course. I became increasingly troubled about how little I knew concerning proper training and care for our children. Finally,

I decided I would go and miss the couple's retreat. I broke the news to my wife and called Rosemead to register for the course. On February 8, I departed for Los Angeles.

When I arrived at Rosemead Graduate School of Psychology, I discovered that my fears were real. Prior to the first week of this two-week course, I was like most preachers, skeptical of psychologists and psychology. After completing the various tests, it became clear to me that psychology was part of God's gift to man. No one could doubt their test scores. Those who were honest and willing took full advantage of the resources that were available at the campus and received the help they needed to confront some of their weaknesses.

For me the course was a real eye-opener. The class was made up of ministers from across the country, as well as foreign missionaries from as far away as Taiwan and China. We were all from different nationalities and races. Some were pastors, some missionaries, and some chaplains in the military. Our qualifications varied; some had degrees from different colleges and universities. It was a good sampling of ministers, missionaries, and their spouses. Group sessions were part of the course, and I think I learned as much from the group sessions as I did in the lectures.

Each person shared what was on his heart. Whether in the pastorate, on the mission field, or in

Forgiveness: The Key to Divine Release

the chaplaincy, we were all convinced that every Christian, regardless of his or her calling in the ministry, is a human being and subject to temptations, fears, and weaknesses.

As a pastor, I have often quoted Hebrews 4:15: "For we have not an high priest which cannot be touched with the feeling of our infirmities; but was in all points tempted like as we are, yet without sin." I believe we have failed to visualize this text when we look for God's help with our own situations. We do not hesitate to remind the Lord that He was tempted in all points as we are, but when it comes to someone else, we forget the end of the verse, "yet without sin." Jesus was a worthy sacrifice for our sins because He qualified as the sinless Son of God. Those who are called to be pastors are not called because they are without sin or a sinful nature.

Pastors, missionaries, and chaplains are men and women who are sinners saved by God's grace. They need His forgiveness as well as the forgiveness of their spouse, children, uncles, aunts, grandparents, congregants, coworkers, and friends.

The apostle John includes himself in this saying:

This then is the message which we have heard of Him, and declare unto you, that God is light, and in Him is no darkness at all. If we say that we have fellowship with him, and walk in darkness, we lie, and do not the truth: but if we walk in the light, as he is in the light, we have fellowship one with another, and the blood of Jesus Christ His Son cleanseth us from all sin. If we say that we have no sin, we deceive ourselves, and the truth is not in us. If we confess our sins, He is faithful and just to forgive us our sins, and to cleanse us from all unrighteousness. If we say that we have not sinned, we make Him a liar, and His word is not in us (1 John 1:5-10).

John makes these points: (a) God is light and in Him is no darkness whatsoever. (b) If we are children of God and in fellowship with Him, we will not walk in darkness or live in habitual sin. (c) As children of light, we walk in the light as He is in the light. As we have fellowship one with another, the blood of Jesus Christ, His Son, cleanses us from all sin. (The word *cleanses* means continuous cleansing, and the ones who walk in the light and in fellowship with other believers need it.) (d) If we say that we have no sin, we are only deceiving ourselves.

To emphasize that fact, John says that the truth is not in us. Nevertheless, if we confess our sins (plural), God is faithful and just to forgive us our sins and to cleanse us from all unrighteousness. Why would God be just to forgive us? David, the psalmist, tells us, "For He knoweth our frame; He remembereth that we are dust" (Ps. 103:14). That is why He does not deal with us after our sins, or reward us according to our iniquities. If God dealt with us based on our iniquities, which of us would be able to stand?

Forgiveness: The Key to Divine Release

John concluded his writing on forgiveness in verse 10 by saying, "If we say that we have not sinned, we make Him a liar, and His word is not in us." In chapter 2, John continues, "My little children, these things write I unto you, that ye sin not" (1 Jn. 2:1a). In other words, God does not want us to sin, but if anyone does sin, he has an advocate with the Father—Jesus Christ.

When God made provision through the blood of Jesus Christ for forgiveness, it did not exclude Christian leaders. He provided forgiveness for all Christians. This includes pastors, missionaries, and chaplains. Therefore, if God knew that pastors needed forgiveness, shouldn't we be willing to forgive them too? Before we look at areas of unforgiveness Christians have held in their hearts toward pastors, I want you to consider the sins of these men in the Scriptures:

Adam—created sinless by God with the privilege of living in a sinless environment. He was given a sinless wife and had the privilege of fellowship with the Lord Jehovah face to face every day. Did he maintain sinlessness? Was he forgiven by God?

Abraham—called directly by God to leave his hometown and his family to follow God. Fearing for his life, he was willing to exchange his wife for his life. Later he failed to trust in God's plan for a son, producing a son through a substitute wife, Hagar.

Abraham made a big mistake when he agreed to have a relationship with Hagar. Did Abraham, the father of faith, sin and need forgiveness?

Moses—Pharaoh signed a death warrant condemning Moses to death before he was born, but God had also signed a warrant that said he must live. Moses, as an adult, murdered an Egyptian. Is murder not a sin? What of his disobedience to God in striking the rock? Did he receive forgiveness?

Joshua—another great leader chosen by God to lead his people after the death of Moses. After the feat of crossing the Jordan and defeating Jericho, he was deceived by the Gibeonites and made a covenant with them against God's wishes. If he were a pastor or the superintendent of a large denomination today, I am sure he would have been asked to resign. If it were you, would you have forgiven him?

David—a man after God's own heart. He was handpicked by God as a shepherd boy to be king over his people. He was a man who sought after God, but one day David saw a pretty woman taking a bath and this mighty warrior, with a heart for God, fell into sin. Not only did he violate the woman, he was also responsible for her husband's death. Later he disobeyed God by numbering the people and thousands died because of God's judgment for what he did.

Would David have found forgiveness in the Church today? What of all the others whom I have

Forgiveness: The Key to Divine Release

not mentioned? Would your congregation be willing to forgive them? What of a man like Peter, who denied his Master three times? Jesus forgave him, and on the Day of Pentecost he was the spokesman who brought the good news to the assembly. As a result, 3,000 souls became members of the Kingdom. Would Peter have found forgiveness in today's Church?

Throughout the New Testament, men who were filled with the Holy Ghost also made mistakes. Paul and Barnabas, men filled with the Holy Spirit, the first missionaries chosen by the Holy Spirit, could not agree and parted company. This all happened because Paul was not prepared to forgive John Mark for his failure.

Pastors are only human; every one of us makes mistakes or sins either by commission or omission. We are admonished to take heed lest we think we are standing when, in fact, we are falling (see 1 Cor. 10:12). I think the apostle Paul addressed this truth in the Book of Romans too. Speaking of the two natures within man, he wrote:

I find then a law, that, when I would do good, evil is present with me. For I delight in the law of God after the inward man: but I see another law in my members, warring against the law of my mind, and bringing me into captivity to the law of sin which is in my members. O, wretched man that I am! who shall deliver me from the body of this death? I thank God through Jesus

Forgiving Your Pastor

Christ our Lord. So then with the mind I myself serve the law of God; but with the flesh the law of sin (Romans 7:21-25).

We all have a job in the process of forgiving our leaders. We must be willing to accept their repentance and demonstrate God's love and mercy through the process of godly restoration. Paul writes, "Brethren, if a man be overtaken in a fault, ye which are spiritual, restore such an one in the spirit of meekness; considering thyself, lest thou also be tempted" (Gal. 6:1).

The pastor has a greater responsibility to walk worthy of the calling to which he has been called of God and to be an example for others by his word, conduct, love, spirit, faith, and purity (see 1 Tim. 4:12). A pastor is called to be a spiritual leader, but as a person, he might be remiss in performing his duties. He may forget to recognize a helper during the vote of thanks—often the person who did the most work. Instead of securing a lasting friendship, his oversight produces a life-long enemy.

A pastor may find himself on poor terms with someone because he fails to place a person in a responsible position. Often he cannot get a release from God for this person, but the damage is done because of false perceptions. Pastors are also judged wrongfully and make enemies because of a sermon. Often pastors listen to stories about congregants and

Forgiveness: The Key to Divine Release

use them as a topic for their sermons (I believe these pastors are in the minority).

Does a fountain send forth at the same place sweet and bitter water? (See James 3:11.) The answer is obvious—it cannot. Even so, a pastor who is under the anointing of the Holy Spirit cannot bring forth from the Holy Spirit and at the same time bring forth from the flesh. For a pastor to make his ears a bin for garbage is to block his ear to the Holy Spirit. Sooner or later, he will find out that he is better off listening to the Holy Spirit. Only then will his preaching be anointed by the Spirit of God.

Anointed preaching brings forth the result God intended. Sermons that emanate from the flesh cannot please God. Pastors called of the Lord will want to please God first. After all, it was God who called them into the ministry. When the Holy Spirit flows through your pastor, you will receive the instruction you need. The *Word* is a two-edged sword that both cuts and heals. Cutting causes pain and pain is not pleasant, but in the end, you will become more like Christ. This should be your desire. Do not let what is intended for your good work to the contrary.

When God gave Jeremiah a message for the people of his day, they became angry at him. He was simply speaking forth what the Lord had given to him. Likewise, do not be angry at your pastor for preaching God's word. Even if you believe that someone spoke to him about you, accept it as from the Lord and let your spirit be pure.

Pastors are men and women saved by God's grace and chosen by Him to shepherd His people. As with all Christians, they must seek to be perfect like Him who has called them. Nevertheless, they still need our forgiveness. The greatness of our spirituality is in our ability to forgive as we desire to be forgiven.

Chapter 12

Forgiveness and the Church

I believe that the most misunderstood group of people in the world today are Christians—including me. I think this is particularly true as it relates to problems that occur among members of any one church, or the Body of Christ as a whole.

Someone has described the Church as "the only army that shoots its wounded." This is probably an understatement. The Church today is filled with unforgiveness—yet we come to church and sing, "O how I love Jesus, because He first loved me." We forget that when He first loved us, no good thing was in any of us. Not one of us deserved His forgiveness. We had wronged Him even before we were conceived in

Forgiveness: The Key to Divine Release

our mother's womb. Yet He forgave us and removed our sins as far as the east is from the west. Not only did He remove our sins beyond the reach of anyone, He buried them in the sea of forgetfulness, never to remember them again. (See Psalm 103:12.)

When He removes our sins, it is forever. No longer does He hold sins against us. His actions toward us are never influenced by what we did in the past. It is not a new page in an old book. It is a new page in a new book, a completely new life, a new relationship. The old life has passed away in the sea of God's forgiveness.

Jesus did not die for people who were perfect, nor did He come to call perfect people to follow Him. He came because He knew we needed forgiveness. We did not deserve His forgiveness, but He looked beyond our faults and saw our need. Jesus' prayer, as recorded in John 17:14, said, "I have given them Thy word; and the world hath hated them, because they are not of the world, even as I am not of the world." We are not of this world. We are of God and the nature of God is forgiveness. Jesus forgave even after His own disciples rejected Him. As our example, He has shown us the way of true victory.

While Jesus was in this world, He too experienced difficulty. At His birth there was no room at the inn. King Herod heard of His birth and His parents were forced to flee with Him across the very rough and

Forgiveness and the Church

rugged terrain of Israel, across the hot, sandy deserts to Egypt.

The chief priests and scribes of Israel realized that the Anointed One, the Messiah, the Prince of Peace, had been born. It was they who had notified King Herod of Jesus' birthplace in Bethlehem of Judea. For thus it was written by the prophet,

But thou, Bethlehem Ephratah, though thou be little among the thousands of Judah, yet out of thee shall He come forth unto Me that is to be ruler in Israel; whose goings forth have been from of old, from everlasting (Micah 5:2).

As Jesus grew older and began His ministry, His problems multiplied. The people of His own nation and especially the leaders were relentless in their efforts to stop His ministry.

They wanted to find a reason to justify killing Him. When they could not find a reason to get rid of Him, they made up a case against Him, gave Him an unfair trial, and condemned Him to die. Pontius Pilate, the governor, offered them the option of releasing Jesus or the criminal Barabbas. They chose the criminal.

Why did Jesus have to suffer so much at the hands of His own people? Was He deserving of their evil thoughts and deeds? Jesus prayed for these very

Forgiveness: The Key to Divine Release

people, "Father, forgive them; for they know not what they do" (Lk. 23:34).

Jesus also prayed to the Father that we may be one with Him, "…as Thou, Father, art in Me, and I in Thee, that they also may be one in Us: that the world may believe that Thou has sent Me" (Jn. 17:21). Two cannot claim to be one when unforgiveness is present. Jesus made that clear.

Ye have heard that it hath been said, Thou shalt love thy neighbour, and hate thine enemy. But I say unto you, Love your enemies, bless them that curse you, do good to them that hate you, and pray for them which despitefully use you, and persecute you; that ye may be the children of your Father which is in heaven: for He maketh His sun to rise on the evil and on the good, and sendeth rain on the just and on the unjust. For if ye love them which love you, what reward have ye? do not even the publicans the same? And if ye salute your brethren only, what do ye more than others? do not even the publicans so? Be ye therefore perfect, even as your Father which is in heaven is perfect (Matthew 5:43-48).

It is normal to love those who love us. It is easy to love those who do things the way we like them to be done, whether in speech or action. We find it easy to forgive such people or even to overlook their errors.

Forgiveness and the Church

But when a similar mistake is made by someone whom we do not appreciate, we hold it against the person and use the mistake as an excuse to justify our condemning spirit. Do not be deceived; the Father knows us on the inside. He knows when we have not forgiven someone, even though the person may not realize it. We should go to the Lord in prayer and, with purpose and sincerity, ask Him to give us a forgiving spirit. Even when we find it difficult to forgive, we can draw on Heaven's resources to have the power to forgive everyone.

God's Kingdom depends on forgiveness. During His earthly ministry, Jesus made it quite clear that the world would know Christianity is real when the world can see oneness in the Church. "By this shall all men know that ye are My disciples, if ye have love one to another" (Jn. 13:35). When we refuse to forgive, the Church becomes a poor representation of the Kingdom of God. I believe unforgiveness is the single most important cause for failure in the Church. The Church is made weak and without power because of its failure to offer forgiveness as Jesus demands.

You may claim that you harbor no negative thoughts toward others, but let us examine the facts. In every local church, there are some members who will not serve on a particular committee because of another individual whose spirit runs counter to

Forgiveness: The Key to Divine Release

theirs. Subtle excuses, such as, "I do not feel the Lord wants me to serve in that capacity at this time, maybe later," or "I am praying about it," just serve as covers to shroud their real feelings against the individual.

There are situations between individuals who have sung in the same choir for years, acting as representatives of the Lord Jesus Christ and as ministers of His grace. This unforgiveness exists in almost every aspect of the local church. Still, we pray daily, "Forgive us our sins as we forgive those who are indebted to us" (see Lk. 11:4). I believe with all my heart that the Church of Jesus Christ will only come into its full potential when we, as believers, understand our new nature. Our new nature is that of Christ. He came not to do His own will, but the will of Him who sent Him. Paul tells us, "Therefore if any man be in Christ, he is a new creature [or creation]: old things [the old unforgiving nature] are passed away; behold, all things are become new" (2 Cor. 5:17).

It is clear that if we are in Christ, we have His nature. He showed us His nature, a nature of forgiveness, when He forgave Judas and included him on His team. Jesus admitted that one of His disciples was a devil, one who was not fully committed to Him. Still, He kept working with him to bring him into the new nature. Unfortunately, Judas refused to turn from his greed and it ultimately destroyed him.

Forgiveness and the Church

On the day of judgment, Judas will not be able to say that he sold Jesus for 30 pieces of silver because Jesus had negative feelings toward him. Jesus' infinite love for Judas was expressed when He dipped His hand with him in the dish (see Jn. 13:26). It was the last time that Jesus offered Judas forgiveness. John's Gospel tells us that Jesus loved His own who were in the world, and loved them to the end (see Jn. 13:1). Jesus loved Judas to the end. It was after Judas had dipped his hand in the same dish with Jesus that the devil overtook him and led him to betray Jesus. Up to that moment Judas could have received the forgiveness of Jesus. "And supper being ended, the devil having now put into the heart of Judas Iscariot, Simon's son, to betray him" (Jn. 13:2).

Unforgiveness in the Church has caused many people to turn away from serving the Lord. If you die in unrighteousness, don't think you can use your lack of service or your unforgiving nature as an excuse to deliver you from the penalty of hell.

But when the righteous turneth away from his righteousness, and committeth iniquity, and doeth according to all the abominations that the wicked man doeth, shall he live? All his righteousness that he hath done shall not be mentioned: in his trespass that he hath trespassed, and in his sin that he hath sinned, in them shall he die (Ezekiel 18:24).

Forgiveness: The Key to Divine Release

It is the spiritual state of a person that determines his destiny. We have a responsibility to help each other go all the way with God. The Lord will not hold us guiltless if, by failing to forgive someone, we have caused them to turn away from serving the Lord. Sometimes people confess that it is very difficult to come to service and worship the Lord when there is a matter unresolved between them and someone in the congregation. These people know their behavior is wrong. The Holy Spirit has convicted them about their unforgiveness. They want to make it right because their spirits cannot be blessed when they know they are living in disobedience to the Word of God.

On the other hand, there is the Christian who is aware of his unforgiving nature, but who makes no effort to resolve the unforgiveness that spoils his relationship with others. He is adamant in his resolve and is not swayed by the Word of God to forgive. Such a person cannot feel or sense what the Holy Spirit is saying and is spiritually dead.

Unforgiveness in the Church is not confined to regular members alone. Leaders are guilty of this sickness also. Periodically, I meet with leaders of the Church for a time of sharing. Sometimes, as these sessions proceed, it is apparent to me that a feeling of animosity exists among certain leaders. As the person in charge, I draw on the wisdom of the Holy

Forgiveness and the Church

Spirit to resolve the situation before it explodes. In most cases the root of the problem is an unresolved conflict between the involved leaders. Unforgiveness is a deadly sin that can destroy an entire ministry and, in the process, cause many souls to go to a lost eternity.

It will be interesting to see the results of a survey of the number of churches no longer in existence because of unforgiveness among leaders or among leaders and members. The results might be shocking to all of us. One does not have to look too far to see or hear of a church that was started because of a split within another congregation. The question is not who has sinned—all of us have sinned and come short of the glory of God in one way or the other (see Rom. 3:23).

James 2:1-13 seems to say that certain practices, which go on in almost every church, are very serious offenses to God. Most of us do not see them that way. In almost every assembly there are instances where people are measured by their outward appearance, yet with God there is no respect of persons. Often those who appear more impressive are escorted to a good seat and welcomed more warmly than the casually attired person. Such discriminatory behavior is sinful in the sight of God. Every sin is condemned by God, yet we overlook some and even are unwilling to forgive others. We begin to act as judge and jury concerning acceptable and unacceptable behavior, but we fail to use Jesus as the standard for judgment.

Forgiveness: The Key to Divine Release

Someone has said there is bad in the best of us as well as good in the worst of us. This statement shows the need for forgiveness in every level within the church. Entire ministries have collapsed and ministers have been expelled from the ministries God built, due to unforgiveness. You may argue that if the ministry were of God it would have survived, even though the person whom God used to bring it into being is no longer there. That argument will not stand on its own; neither will the Bible support that belief. God's Word clearly states that without a vision, the people perish (see Prov. 29:18). Leadership is very important because it provides direction to the vision. Israel was chosen by God and every time the nation had a leader who did not follow the Lord, the people backslid and destruction followed.

In First Samuel 2 and 3, we find that Eli had faltered badly. The people followed after their own ways until God's judgment came and the nation was defeated. The word of the Lord was rare in that day and there was a lack of vision. You may think that if Eli had been removed, Israel would have been better off. That is not necessarily true. Samuel was not ready, at the time, to assume the role of prophet. God is the one in charge, and He knows when to remove one and set up another. He does not need our unforgiving spirits and actions to fulfill His purpose for His Church.

God did not deal with Eli on the basis of unforgiveness. On the contrary, He wanted Eli to turn from his erring ways and enjoy His blessings. He did

Forgiveness and the Church

not remove Eli because of one mistake. Only after Eli refused to repent of his evil ways did God remove him and replace him with Samuel.

There is a similar example with Moses and Joshua. Moses made a major blunder, but Joshua did not seek to capitalize on Moses' mistake. He was faithful to Moses until his death and *then* it became time for Joshua to lead the people.

Now after the death of Moses the servant of the Lord it came to pass, that the Lord spake unto Joshua the son of Nun, Moses' minister, saying, Moses My servant is dead; now therefore arise, go over this Jordan, thou, and all this people, unto the land which I do give to them, even to the children of Israel (Joshua 1:1-2).

Joshua did not walk around with unforgiveness against Moses, trying to turn the hearts of the people against him. There were other leaders who tried that—Dathan, Korah, and Abiram. These men harbored negative feelings against Moses because they felt he had taken too much upon himself.

The Bible speaks strongly against this type of division taking place in the Body of Christ as we wait for His imminent return. "Woe be unto the pastors that destroy and scatter the sheep of My pasture! saith the Lord" (Jer. 23:1). The root of these divisions in the Church is unforgiveness, which often results in good members leaving one church for another.

Forgiveness: The Key to Divine Release

They hope they can find something different. They are tired of members leaving, of churches splitting into various groups with the same negative result, and of buildings closing because the remaining members cannot maintain it. They are tired of pastors being dragged through the mud and forced to resign from their ministry. Unforgiveness in the Body of Christ is costing God a great deal, and somebody will have to pay sooner or later.

Unforgiveness is deadly. I pray that everyone of us would depart from it and let the sweet love of Jesus flow freely from within our hearts. I do not know if there is unforgiveness in your heart against a brother or sister in Christ, or if someone harbors negative feelings in his heart for you. If so, make a decision now to go to that person and resolve the problem without delay.

Agreement among church members is vital for positive results. Jesus said that if two of us shall agree as touching anything, it shall be done (see Mt. 18:19). The Church must be united in order to be strong. It also must be properly nourished to do exploits for the glory of God. When God puts an assembly together, it is important that every part be fitly joined together for the free flowing of the Holy Spirit. The nature of God's Church is to move toward maturity so the work of the ministry can go forth and the Body of Christ be edified. We will come into the

Forgiveness and the Church

unity of the faith and of the knowledge of the Son of God, and as creatures perfected by His power, we will grow in stature to the fullness of Christ (see Eph. 4:13).

From whom the whole body fitly joined together and compacted by that which every joint supplieth, according to the effectual working in the measure of every part, maketh increase of the body unto the edifying of itself in love (Ephesians 4:16).

Chapter 13

Forgiving Teachers and Educators

"Be ye followers of me, even as I also am of Christ" (1 Cor. 11:1). This verse can also depict the role of a teacher to his students; teachers are role models to numerous students.

Teachers are significant people too. They have influenced almost every life in the civilized world. The words of the text above give some indication of the impact teachers have on their students. They are responsible for their education, they help form their character, and for many, they are examples of the Christian life style. Unfortunately, some teachers misuse their position and authority, leaving a bitter memory for many people. If you harbor such memories, it

Forgiveness: The Key to Divine Release

is time for you to look past the bitterness, the negative feelings, and the hurt you may feel.

God's plan of education is one where the newborn is taught basic principles from his family. As the Father of Adam, God taught him first; then Adam taught his sons. Education was passed on from the parents to their children, down through the generations. Although the system surely differed from the one we have today, we should not think that our forefathers were any less bright than the best we have today. After all, Adam named all of the plants and animals; Enoch built a city (without a computer, I might add); and Noah built an ark large enough to house two representatives of the animal population of the world. With the knowledge we have received from these men and women, we can see that God's method and process is a good one.

For the child, life was centered around the home and the immediate community. There was less pressure on the child to live up to manufactured standards. The home was a familiar place and this brought a measure of comfort to the child during the learning process. Generally, there was food to eat, clothes to wear, and a loving set of parents to whom the child could turn.

Although we might judge life in those times to be harsh, it had a number of positive advantages that we have abandoned today.

Forgiving Teachers and Educators

Imagine yourself as a young child today. Perhaps this is the scenario you experienced. At first you see the older children (brother, sister, and neighbors) leave for a day at school. Although you can't quite make the connection at this stage in your life, someday your life will change as you enter the education arena. The day will come when your parents begin to talk about the approaching school year, your first year as a student. The excitement begins to build as you try on new "school clothes" or a school uniform. The newness and the fuss make you an instant celebrity with the family.

When the big day finally arrives, you are filled with anticipation. You are the first one out of bed and you dress, careful to get everything in place. As soon as your proud parents finish taking pictures, you bound out the door and into the car.

Finally, the moment you have been waiting for is here, as your father parks the car. You and your parents make your way to the school office where a number of other children are waiting with their parents. The whole scene is chaos. Some children are crying, some screaming, and others objecting to the process. You no longer feel like a celebrity. Instead, you feel more like a victim and you too would like a way out of this entrapment.

As a woman on the other side of a high counter works with stacks of applications, you notice the

Forgiveness: The Key to Divine Release

other parents are busy answering a set of questions. When they are finished, they sign a form and are given directions to various rooms. As they leave, the tears and the screams start again as the children are dragged down the hall.

Then you realize you are next. You are aware of your mother encouraging you by describing how nice your teacher will be and how much you will enjoy school. It is now your turn and the person behind the counter smiles and says, "Hello! What is your name?" As soon as you tell her your name, she greets you personally and welcomes you to the school. Then you are suddenly ignored as your parents go through the "question and answer" sheet. Finally you hear the counter person give directions to your classroom and you start the first of many walks down the hall. This is the first day of your new life as a student.

When you reach your room, you notice a mother trying to leave, but her daughter is clinging to her dress. Hearing her screams, fear comes over you as your parents lead you over to the teacher. There is a moment of confusion as the teacher tries to handle the screaming child and turn her attention to you at the same time. At last she reaches down and takes your hand with a smile as your parents say their good-byes. You feel like your world is caving in as the reality of what is happening hits you. You are about to be separated from home and parents for most of the day, five days out of every week.

134

Forgiving Teachers and Educators

Your head is filled with questions as you try to adjust from your home's secure surroundings, where you could run free, to this more structured environment. From now on you will not be taught in bits and pieces, but in an orderly manner with a definite beginning and end.

It is important for you to have the right concept of school and education. The main goal of the teacher is for you to develop a love for school and learning. So, to make learning fun, you are introduced to various activities aimed at developing eye and hand coordination, fine motor skills, pre-math and pre-reading skills, number concepts, sequencing, and social skills. These activities include cutting, painting, field trips, modeling with clay, physical education, music, and art. With the main goal in mind, your teacher makes sure you enjoy your learning activities. Soon you become fascinated with the learning exercises and before long, school is a wonderful place.

Your apprehensions are now behind you and the trust reserved for your parents is now shared with your teacher. Your world is expanding rapidly as your capacity to learn increases. Each day brings new discoveries and the person responsible for your progress is your teacher. She becomes the center of your learning experience. Each day, when you get home, one of the first questions you are asked is, "What did you learn today?" or "What did your teacher teach you?"

Forgiveness: The Key to Divine Release

Your teacher seems to be as important as your parents. Your parents are responsible for what you wear, what you eat, and where and when you sleep. But when it comes to learning, your teacher is the most important person. She takes time to make sure you understand what she is teaching and she helps you practice your lessons. At the same time she helps you develop confidence and makes you feel comfortable with yourself and with others.

The second year is not the same as the first, and each succeeding year brings new challenges. Kindergarten and grade one deal with the areas of letter recognition by sight and sound, blending of consonants, vowels, reading short vowel words, number recognition, and number concepts. As you move from grade two to grade three, you start asking questions. You no longer accept everything you are taught. You want more information and reasons for why things happen as you have been told. Your teacher is not quite as sweet or gentle as your first teacher. When you challenge his instructions or teaching, he sees you in a different light. You are accused of being rude and disruptive in class. You cannot understand why you are accused of being disruptive when you ask questions about subject matters you do not fully understand. Little by little the affection you developed for your previous teachers begins to wane. It seems as if there is a conspiracy against you as letters

Forgiving Teachers and Educators

are sent home and conferences take place with your parents.

The frustration increases as you are caught between the pressure from your parents at home and your teacher at school. It is as though you are trapped because every time there is a complaint, you seem to lose and your teacher comes out the winner. School becomes a place of conflict and the conflict reaches right into your home. Your parents seem to relate to you only through the eyes of your teacher. Privileges you once enjoyed are tied to your behavior at school and your grades.

At first you try to please your teacher, hoping to improve your standing at school and at home. You stop asking so many questions and you sit quietly and complete all your assignments. Although the scheme seems to bring peace at home, you are frustrated because you know you could improve your performance if you were free to ask questions. To you, your quest for information is important, but your teacher sees it as disruptive. You ask yourself, "Why won't the teacher consider my point of view?" Not only that, but your grades start to suffer because of your confusion about the subject matter. All you hope to do is make it through the year, so you repress your feelings and hold your observations. If you can only finish the year, you will be out of this class.

As the end of the term approaches, you work hard to complete your assignments and prepare for the

Forgiveness: The Key to Divine Release

year-end tests. When the final bell rings you are relieved, because you believe you have done well. At least you have given it the best you could. Confident that you did not do poorly, you look forward to a good report, one that your parents will be proud to review. Each day you wait for the mail to come. Then on the very day your father comes home early, the report arrives. You aren't told that it has come or that the envelope contains a request from the teacher for a conference. As your parents tell you of the meeting over dinner, a little fear comes over you. Then your father says, "I hope you got some A's on your report card." Knowing that you did your best, the fear leaves and you smile and respond with a positive note.

Later that week your parents come home early to prepare for the conference with your teacher. When you arrive at school, your teacher greets your parents cordially and invites them to have a seat. After a brief moment you are asked to step outside, so your teacher can have a private discussion with your parents. It is from this point that things begin to deteriorate. Your teacher makes sure he has your parents on his side by complaining about how you always interrupt him as he teaches and poke fun at him when he does not respond to your interruptions. He assures your parents that you have the potential to do good work and to be a good student. But, he also

Forgiving Teachers and Educators

assures them that you will have to change your ways to achieve these goals.

When the private discussion ends, you go back into the room so they can review your report. You got an "A" for Math, a "B" for Science and English, but "C's" and "F's" in the other areas. Your parents' faces show their disappointment and you wonder, "How can this be true?" Then you see your teacher as he looks at you with a smile that says, "I fixed you now, boy."

You cannot believe what you have just experienced and it hurts inside. Before third grade, teachers were great people. They had captured your love, affection, and trust, but now you see another side to teachers. Teachers can be mean and even dangerous. As you consider the past year and your teacher, you decide this must be an isolated case. Even if this third grade teacher is mean, next year you will start fresh with a brand new teacher. You are sure things will be different.

Unfortunately, you do not know how far your third grade teacher will go to make life miserable for you. It seems he is a good friend of the fourth grade teacher and he fills her in on all the bad things he has accused you of doing. As you enter fourth grade, you realize your new teacher has already made up her mind.

Forgiveness: The Key to Divine Release

Her attitude toward you is decidedly negative. No matter how hard you try, it is not good enough. You believe she is demanding too much from you compared to her demands on the rest of the class. Your worst fears are confirmed when she lets it slip that she has talked with your third grade teacher and knows all about your disruptive ways. Your trust of teachers goes down another notch and you begin to develop more negative feelings toward teachers in general.

You feel that you have never been given a chance to excel. As you grow older, you grow in knowledge too, but your teachers do not seem to be conscious of this fact. As a result, they do not like it when you challenge them. When you do, they treat you like a public enemy. Some teachers have difficulty recognizing bright students, especially if the student is smarter than they are. The failure to identify bright students can cause friction and unnecessary hurt to students. This may have been your dilemma.

In Psalm 119:99, the Psalmist says that he had more understanding than all his teachers. In the verses before and after verse 99, we read of a student who was eager to learn. He had a love for what he was studying—the Word of God. He also considered carefully what he was studying. In verse 98 he claims that he was wiser than his enemies. A man's enemies will use any means to hurt him and his testimony, but the fact that his enemies could not outsmart him confirms that he was a wise man. In

Forgiving Teachers and Educators

claiming greater wisdom than his teachers, he was not spouting empty claims.

A student who likes to study and desires to know more than what he is being taught can get himself in trouble with his teacher. Most people who deliberately misbehave and get caught do not become too upset when they are punished because they know they deserve the punishment. When a student is punished unjustly or singled out for special condemnation, he grows bitter and irate at the injustice of those in authority.

One reason for any unforgiveness and resentment you may feel toward one or more of your teachers could be their prejudice toward the color of your skin. Unfortunately, this is a major stumbling block in the lives of many students. You might say, "How could I forgive a teacher who insulted me time after time for no other reason than the color of my skin?" Perhaps you were constantly reminded that you were too dumb to go very far. You could have been often treated unfairly, seeing other students getting higher test scores on poorer work. Maybe there were times when you felt like giving up, but somebody kept encouraging you. To everyone's surprise but your own, you held on and made it through to the end.

Many teachers have hurt students. You would not be alone with this problem. I met someone a number

Forgiveness: The Key to Divine Release

of years ago who told me of his experience at school. He said he could not say why he was hated by some of his teachers, but he was taken a number of times to the principal's office and often received punishment. Many times he was told that he was no good and would not amount to anything. He said he heard those words so many times he almost believed them until, one day, he met a teacher who told him he could succeed. Those words changed his outlook of himself. His heart was stirred by someone who loved him even though he did not have the same skin color.

That teacher continued to encourage him and today the Lord has blessed the former student to be the president of his organization. This organization now owns the school building where he attended school. The principal's office is now his office and he sits in the very same chair in which his principal sat.

You don't know what the future will bring because God holds the future. God has said, "...Vengeance belongeth unto Me, I will recompense, saith the Lord..." (Heb. 10:30). As you learn to forgive those who have wronged or hurt you, you give the Lord the authority to handle your situations. When you carry unforgiveness, you tie the Lord's hand from working on your behalf. True victory will come, as you are willing to let go and allow the Lord to handle the situation. You may find it difficult to forgive your teacher for the hurts you carry, but remember you

Forgiving Teachers and Educators

can only receive God's blessing when you have the courage to forgive as He has commanded in His Word. "If you do not forgive men their trespasses against you, neither will your Father who is in Heaven forgive you your trespasses."

You cannot afford to allow teachers who disliked you to keep you in bondage with their negative statements and actions. God has made you a precious person for His glory and honor. He desires that you fulfill His purpose by forgiving those teachers you find hard to forgive.

Chapter 14

Forgiveness and Your Job

As you go through life, you will meet and develop relationships with a number of different people. Regardless of the relationship, the need to forgive is paramount if the relationship is to grow and mature. On the other hand, a refusal to forgive will result in the destruction of any relationship. Outside of the family and close friends, every relationship begins under varying circumstances. The opportunity for a number of relationships opens up when you enter the job market or change from one job to another.

The reason I use the word *opportunity* is many people seldom take time to develop relationships with their coworkers. The reason for that reluctance may be the result of past hurts endured at the hands of coworkers, a supervisor, or a boss.

Forgiveness: The Key to Divine Release

Put yourself in the shoes of someone who has been out of a job for a time. The bills are piling up and the creditors are calling. As you sit down for dinner you can feel the indigestion growing inside. You feel helpless and frustrated after spending another day pounding the sidewalk. The unemployment check does not cover even the basic necessities. In addition, you were treated like a beggar at the unemployment office instead of a person who worked and contributed to the unemployment insurance you now depend upon for your subsistence.

In most cases, you are desperate for a job, any job, and you have no time to spend cultivating a new friendship. What is important to you is getting a job so the bills can be paid and the bill collectors stopped. To add to your frustration, each interview seems to be a dead end. You have heard the words, "We are still interviewing, but as soon as we make a decision we will call you," so often they sound like a broken record. You know they really mean, "Don't call us, we'll call you."

About the time you are sure you will never work again, the phone rings and the employment agency happily announces that you have been hired by a large corporation. They go on to explain that it is not exactly what you are looking for, but they expect a position in your field to open soon. Meanwhile, they encourage you to take this job. At least you can get your foot in the door.

Forgiveness and Your Job

You take down the information and prepare for the interview. The only thing on your mind is to get the job and pay your bills. To your delight, everything goes smoothly and you are given the position. The compensation is not bad and everyone you meet seems wonderful. You are looking forward to your new job.

The cliché, "Come see me and come live with me are two different things," is always true. When persons are first introduced, the idea is to make a good impression. After a while, the true nature of each individual begins to emerge. *Temperaments* differ and after working with people for a while, most realize their first impressions were not entirely accurate.

You yourself experience this at your new job. You begin to wonder whom you can trust. You are the new employee, and you get a number of different reactions. Some assume you will only be there a short while, so they keep the relationship friendly. Others assume you may prove a better worker than they are and see you as a threat.

The boss looks upon you as someone he can control and, as the new worker, someone easier to manipulate. He is nice to you and you feel this is the best working relationship you have enjoyed in all of your working years. What you do not realize is the courtship will come to an end. *Courtship* is an appropriate word to describe your circumstances because

Forgiveness: The Key to Divine Release

that is just what your job is. Your coworkers court you for your allegiance; your boss, on the other hand, would like you to be his eyes and ears. Even though you realize what is happening, your most important concern is to keep your job and pay off your debts. The tension created by your need and by the circumstances motivates you to walk the tightrope and make sure no side can claim victory. You decide to treat everyone with equal respect.

Two years pass and the bills are almost paid. There are no more furniture payments; the last coupon is in the envelope ready to be mailed. The tension eases as life becomes more manageable. Things that you placed on the back burner suddenly begin to move to the front. You remember that this job you took was not what you were looking for at the time. Your status with the company has not changed and there has been no indication that any other opportunities are open to you. Dissatisfaction moves in and you begin to think of making a change.

Before you realize it, your attitude changes toward your job. You are not as punctual as you were in the beginning and your coworkers notice the trend in your work habits. They know you will either be a friend of the boss or will join forces with them against management. They are sure you cannot continue to be the nice guy indefinitely. You are at a crossroads and must make a decision. Your boss,

Forgiveness and Your Job

sensing your situation, reasserts his authority to get you under control.

Then, by coincidence, a position in the company opens up and you decide to apply for it. You need a recommendation from your boss if you are to have any chance at the promotion. You shift gears again because you know you will have to be nice to the boss to get his help. Of course, your coworkers see what you are doing and they are not happy with your ambitions. They start to give you the cold shoulder, which makes you uncomfortable. The situation is difficult where you are and you hope the new position will be yours and your problems resolved. Just when it looks like you have the job in the bag, your boss goes against you and you lose out.

Now what do you do? All of a sudden, the wonderful people in the company are no longer so wonderful. Your boss has let you down, your friends are not speaking to you, and the confidence you had toward the new job has been smashed. You are angry at your boss for not coming through for you, and you are angry with your coworkers for treating you badly.

Going to work is no longer a joy. It is only a means to pay your bills. Each day brings more and more frustration, anger, and resentment. You would like to leave, but if you do, you fear that you will go right back into the hole from which you are about to crawl. So life becomes a daily struggle and you know something must give. You must find a way out soon, for

Forgiveness: The Key to Divine Release

each day you are there anger is building in your heart. The relationships with your boss and your co-workers are deteriorating, and you know it is just a matter of time before you will be terminated.

Each day, as you prepare for work, you wonder what is in store for you. Will you still have a job or will today be the last? Then one morning as you start out of the house, something stirs in your spirit. You are certain something is about to happen. Sure enough, one thing after another goes wrong.

You need to leave home at 7:30 a.m. to make it to your job on time, but today it is 7:40 and you are still not out the door. By the time you get to the train station, you have missed your last chance to get to work on time. When the next train arrives, you rationalize your situation and decide that it isn't so bad to be 15 or 20 minutes late. Suddenly the train comes to a screeching halt. Someone pulled the emergency brake because a passenger is sick. Your 15-minute delay now looks more like 30 minutes or more.

When you finally arrive at work, you are a full hour late. Your boss calls you into his office and tells you to clean out your desk because your services are no longer needed. As you walk toward your work area, several things rush through your mind and your anger increases. As you pack your things, you glance toward your coworkers, looking for any sign of sympathy. The whole experience becomes more painful as you take your last step out of the door. Tears

Forgiveness and Your Job

begin to flow down your face and your vision blurs. You do not know whether you should go home or to the unemployment office. As hatred or loathing continues to rage within, you can't get the whole experience out of your mind. You hate your boss and your former coworkers. You see them as betraying you and you are sorry you ever got to know them.

Your prayers are answered when the employment agency calls to tell you they have a good position doing the type of work you requested. Your confidence begins to return and you bury the anger you have carried since you lost your job. The interview goes well and you are hired. At first everything works in your favor, but you decide to keep people at a distance. Because of your last experience, you are afraid to trust anyone and so devote all of your energy to your work. You decide that as long as you are an asset to your employer, he will always need you. It is your way of suppressing the anger that you still carry against your former employers. Unfortunately, you are only deceiving yourself. You can't go through life harboring anger and resentment. You must confront your hurt and forgive those who have hurt you.

Does this scenario sound familiar? Relationships gone sour on the job result in hurt among workers on every level. When Paul wrote to Timothy, he was addressing the problems created by a working relationship.

And that from a child thou hast known the holy scriptures, which are able to make thee wise

Forgiveness: The Key to Divine Release

unto salvation through faith which is in Christ Jesus. All scripture is given by inspiration of God, and is profitable for doctrine, for reproof, for correction, for instruction in righteousness: that the man of God may be perfect, thoroughly furnished unto all good works (2 Timothy 3:15-17).

Scripture is profitable because we can learn to free ourselves from the bondage we create if we are wise and follow its instructions as they are given. Through faith in Jesus Christ and obedience to God's Word, we will learn to forgive those who have wronged us on the job. The first lesson is to forgive all who have wronged us or caused us to carry hurt in our hearts.

The Book of Philemon is a classic example of the employer-worker dispute. Philemon was well off and had a number of servants. He was saved through Paul's ministry, and we learn from Paul's letter to him that Onesimus, one of his servants, had stolen from him and fled to Rome. While in Rome, he heard the gospel and was saved. When Paul learned what Onesimus had done to Philemon, he took the necessary steps to remove the negative feelings that existed between Philemon and Onesimus. He encouraged Onesimus to retrace his steps and make things right between himself and his master, and he encouraged Philemon to receive his servant in the spirit of Christ. Paul was willing to risk his own friendship

Forgiveness and Your Job

with Philemon to bring about a reconciliation between these two individuals.

Wherefore, though I might be much bold in Christ to enjoin thee that which is convenient, yet for love's sake I rather beseech thee, being such an one as Paul the aged, and now also a prisoner of Jesus Christ. I beseech thee for my son Onesimus, whom I have begotten in my bonds: which in time past was to thee unprofitable, but now profitable to thee and to me: whom I have sent again: thou therefore receive him, that is, mine own bowels: whom I would have retained with me, that in thy stead he might have ministered unto me in the bonds of the gospel: but without thy mind would I do nothing; that thy benefit should not be as it were of necessity, but willingly. For perhaps he therefore departed for a season, that thou shouldest receive him for ever; not now as a servant, but above a servant, a brother beloved, specially to me, but how much more unto thee, both in the flesh, and in the Lord? If thou count me therefore a partner, receive him as myself. If he hath wronged thee, or oweth thee ought, put that on mine account; I Paul have written it with mine own hand, I will repay it: albeit I do not say to thee how thou owest unto me even thine own self besides. Yea, brother, let me have joy of thee in the Lord: refresh my bowels in the Lord. Having confidence in thy obedience I

Forgiveness: The Key to Divine Release

wrote unto thee, knowing that thou wilt also do more than I say. But withal prepare me also a lodging: for I trust that through your prayers I shall be given unto you (Philemon 8-20).

We can see from Paul's letter the importance he placed on forgiveness between these two men in Christ. Paul was willing to risk his own relationship with the "employer," Philemon, to help him understand that he cannot have a fruitful life in God if he cannot forgive his servant Onesimus. It would have been easy for Paul to keep Onesimus with him in Rome and prevent Philemon from having to confront the issue. However, the apostle was not willing to release his friend from doing what the Word of God requires.

If you have a negative feeling against anyone, go to that person and discuss it. You need to make it right, not following the world's system, but godly principles. If it were not for Paul, Philemon might have had Onesimus arrested and put in prison for his wicked act. This may have given him some sort of satisfaction, but he would not have resolved the problem with their relationship. Onesimus would have always been referred to as a thief and a prisoner. This is the way the law works. It condemns and gets even, but God's way is to remove what stands in the way of a healthy relationship.

Paul appealed to Philemon on the basis of his Christian responsibility to love his servant as Christ

Forgiveness and Your Job

has loved him. One final thing remained to repair the breach that caused the problem: making restitution of the money Onesimus stole. Paul appealed to Philemon on this issue by citing a higher law, the law of forgiveness (see Mt. 18:25-27).

Paul, in asking Philemon to do what Jesus laid out as righteous, went on to say that if he would not wipe away the debt for his sake alone, to put it on Paul's account. I like this advice, "Charge it to me, Philemon." To persuade him to do the righteous thing, Paul reminded his friend that he, Philemon, had stolen a whole lot more than he would ever have been able to repay and God forgave him all his debt.

Paul would have been greatly disappointed if Philemon had rejected his admonition because he knew if his friend could not forgive his servant, then he could not receive God's forgiveness. The one act is contingent on the other. So, in effect, Paul said to his friend, "I am holding my breath; let me have joy of you in the Lord. Refresh my heart in the Lord" (see Philem. 20).

Then Paul makes one final point. I believe the import of his appeal was this: "If you want to see me released from prison, then you pray for my release. Remember, though, if you have unforgiveness in your heart, God will not hear and answer your prayer. So you decide if I am important to you. If you know for certain that your heart is right toward God

Forgiveness: The Key to Divine Release

because you have forgiven your brother Onesimus for what he did to you, then you can expect God to hear and answer your prayer for my release. Then put feet to your prayers and prepare me a lodging" (see Philem. 21-22).

Remember, if you do not forgive those with whom you work, neither will your Father who is in Heaven forgive you. Maybe you feel that since you are no longer on the same job with those whom you had conflicts, it is okay to ignore the hurt and unforgiveness. According to the Word of God, you need to retrace your steps and, if possible, contact these coworkers. Witness to them of your faith and forgive them for what they did to you.

They may not be willing to forgive you or to change the way they think of you. They may not even understand why you made the effort to find them. Remember, you are not responsible for what they do or think in their hearts toward you, but it is important that you be in right standing with the Lord Jesus Christ.

Chapter 15

Forgiving Your Friends

In the best of situations, the relationship with a friend should be free of hurts and disappointments. However, it is not realistic to expect your friend never to hurt you. Still, Jesus placed a high premium on friendship.

Jesus and His Friends

Henceforth I call you not servants; for the servant knoweth not what his lord doeth: but I have called you friends; for all things that I have heard of My Father I have made known unto you (John 15:15).

From Jesus' statement we can see that as a friend to His disciples, He kept nothing back from them. He developed a relationship with them that was stronger than either the parent/child or brother/sister

Forgiveness: The Key to Divine Release

relationship. Matthew records an event that confirms Jesus' position on the importance of His friends.

> *While He yet talked to the people, behold, His mother and His brethren stood without, desiring to speak with Him. Then one said unto Him, Behold, Thy mother and Thy brethren stand without, desiring to speak with Thee. But He answered and said unto him that told Him, Who is My mother? and who are My brethren? And He stretched forth His hand toward His disciples, and said, Behold My mother and My brethren!* (Matthew 12:46-49).

In most cases, your friend knows more about you than your parents or your brother or sister. Your friend is your trusted companion. This friendship is a relationship built over a period of time. Little by little you let someone into your life until one day you feel sure the person is your most trusted confidant. Situations and circumstances that you have shared with no one else, you begin to reveal to your best friend.

You had no option to choose your parents or your siblings. They are your family and you were born with them. Your family experience may not have been all that great. You may have been the least favorite child or you may have had a number of conflicts with your brothers and sisters. Because you were the one who excelled in the home, you were the

Forgiving Your Friends

object of envy and sibling rivalry. When your parents failed to recognize the problem, you had no alternative but to seek solace outside of your home environment. You couldn't choose your family, but you could choose your friends.

Jesus was despised by His own brothers and sisters too. He understood what it was to seek friendship outside His home. The Scriptures show Him to be a loner. At the age of 12, when He was in the temple, it was three days before any of His family realized He was missing. When He went to be baptized, no family member was with Him. After His baptism, He was walking alone when some of John's disciples decided they wanted to be His friends and follow Him.

Even after He told them "the foxes have holes, and the birds of the air have nests; but the Son of man hath not where to lay His head" (Mt. 8:20), they still wanted to follow Him. His circle of friends developed by choice. Either He chose them or they chose to follow Him.

You choose to have a friend because every human being has a need to share his or her inner person with someone. Even though it is rare, some people find that person in their father, mother, brother, or sister. Most people find such a friend outside of their home. A close friend occupies a special place in your heart, which makes you feel free to share and to do things together as much as possible. You expect the best from your friend. The disciples of Jesus devoted

Forgiveness: The Key to Divine Release

most of their time to Him. They slept, ate, walked, and talked with Him; they knew almost everything about Him. You too probably spend a lot of time with your friend.

David and Jonathan

We find another example of friendship in the Old Testament. This friendship involved two very important young men, Jonathan and David. One was the king's son and the other was the king-elect. These young men were drawn together because they had similar likes and dislikes—they both loved God and the nation of Israel. Together they carried out God's plan for delivering the people from the hands of the enemies. On two separate occasions, Jonathan and David saw their nation in a state of helplessness against the Philistines and believed God would do something to deliver His people. Even though one was a prince and the other a shepherd boy, God used them both to bring about victory to their nation.

The circumstance that brought these two young men together was unusual. Jonathan's father, King Saul, needed someone with musical abilities. David was proficient with the harp, so he was the one chosen to play for Saul. The music soothed the king and eased his headaches. David served the king until the nation was once again at war. Then he was released and so returned home to take care of his father's sheep. Meanwhile, Jonathan went off to battle.

160

Forgiving Your Friends

God had other plans for David, however. He used this war to bring David and Jonathan together. David's father, Jesse, sent him to carry food to his brothers who were on the battlefield. When he arrived, he heard the champion of the Philistines, Goliath, calling out and mocking the army of Israel. He defied the armies of Israel and called them to send a man to fight him. Out of fear, neither Saul nor one member of his army was willing to accept the challenge.

David, on the other hand, knew God was able to give him victory over Goliath. David spoke to the man who stood by him and said, "What shall be done for the man who kills this Philistine, and takes away the reproach from Israel?" (see 1 Sam. 17:26) He could not understand how an uncircumcised Philistine could defy the armies of the living God. David's brothers criticized him for speaking as he did, but David said to his brother, "Is there not a cause?"

As I mentioned earlier, there is often one member of a family that excels and is envied by his brothers or sisters. David found himself in such a position. First he was chosen to be Saul's personal musician, which did not sit well with his brothers. Now he was questioning their courage and challenging Goliath. This incensed his brothers. Still, he knew that God's will was more important than appeasing his brothers' wrath.

When Saul heard what David had said, he sent for him. David told the king, "Let no man's heart fail

Forgiveness: The Key to Divine Release

because of him; thy servant will go and fight with this Philistine." Saul replied, "Thou art but a youth, and he a man of war from his youth." David then described the way he had defended his father's sheep by slaying first a lion and then a bear. David ended with, "And this uncircumcised Philistine shall be as one of them, seeing he hath defied the armies of the living God. ...Moreover, the Lord, who delivered me out of the paw of the lion, and out of the paw of the bear, He will deliver me out of the hand of this Philistine." Saul told him, "Go, and the Lord be with thee." (See First Samuel 17:31-37.)

After David defeated Goliath, the friendship of David and Jonathan was solidified.

And it came to pass, when he had made an end of speaking unto Saul, that the soul of Jonathan was knit with the soul of David, and Jonathan loved him as his own soul. And Saul took him that day, and would let him go no more home to his father's house. Then Jonathan and David made a covenant, because he loved him as his own soul. And Jonathan stripped himself of the robe that was upon him, and gave it to David, and his garments, even to his sword, and to his bow, and to his girdle (1 Samuel 18:1-4).

True Friendship

What is true friendship? We can see that Jonathan and David were both from different backgrounds— one was rich and the other poor; one a prince and the

Forgiving Your Friends

other a peasant. So friendship, first, does not require people to be from the same social status or to have equal amounts of money. Secondly, we see that friendship is a knitting together of souls. It is a relationship that is not based on physical attraction or family relationships.

Have you ever been asked to describe your relationship with your closest friend? You might have said, "I really cannot explain how I feel toward that person. There isn't any specific thing that I like; it is just the person. There is something about him that makes me want to be with him." It is your soul knitting to the soul of that person.

Thirdly, true friends covenant with each other. Jonathan and David made a covenant or a solemn agreement that was not written on paper, but on each of their hearts. Basically, this covenant says, "I will be there for you in the good times as well as the hard times. We will swim or sink together and you can count on me. I will never betray your trust."

Fourthly, we see that Jonathan gave himself to his friend. Jonathan stripped himself of his robe and gave it to David along with his garments, sword, bow, and belt. He demonstrated that nothing is worth so much to keep it from his friend. Jonathan did what he could to make David his equal.

Friendship Is Often Tested

The friendship between these two men was severely tested time and time again. After David defeated

Forgiveness: The Key to Divine Release

Goliath, the people wrote a song that sang his praises. It angered Saul that David received more recognition than he did. He began to envy David from that day forward. Twice David barely escaped with his life.

Eventually, David became Saul's enemy and was forced to run away and hide. Saul had given instructions to Jonathan and his servants to kill David, but Jonathan refused to violate his covenant with David. He told David of the decree and described a secret place where he would be safe from Saul. He was a true friend to David and protected him on every side.

We would all like to have a friend like Jonathan. When we are true to our friends, the last thing we expect is for our friends to hurt us. Jesus understood the importance of friendship and the seriousness of a friend's failure. Even so, He commanded us to forgive our best friend when he or she lets us down. When a friend fails to honor our friendship, it hurts. In Psalm 41, David wrote of the failure of a friend.

Mine enemies speak evil of me, When shall he die, and his name perish? And if he come to see me, he speaketh vanity: his heart gathereth iniquity to itself; when he goeth abroad, he telleth it. All that hate me whisper together against me: against me do they devise my hurt. An evil disease, say they, cleaveth fast unto him: and now that he lieth he shall rise up no more.

Forgiving Your Friends

Yea, mine own familiar friend, in whom I trusted, which did eat of my bread, hath lifted up his heel against me (Psalm 41:5-9).

You would call such a friend a "turncoat." What did your friend do to you? Did he speak evil about you to someone else? Were you in a business venture together and your friend stole your money? Someone once said, "It is only your friend who can hurt you." This is true to a point because in most cases, you would not permit someone you are uncomfortable with to get close to you.

I do not know what your friend has done to you. Remember Jesus understands and cares, and He is the One who commands you to forgive those who have hurt you. Some of you may have developed what you thought to be a genuine friendship with someone at work. For a number of years you worked and shared your lives with each other. You looked out for the good of your friend, but the time came when the company decided to promote him to a supervisor's position. Your friend suddenly became your adversary and tried, on several occasions, to get you in trouble.

A friend is only a friend when your friendship can stand the test of daily life and association. A person can be a genuine friend with the best of intentions, but if he or she has a problem with finances, that friend can hurt you. The problem would be too great

Forgiveness: The Key to Divine Release

and the friendship too weak to withstand the test. Or like the person who received the promotion, you may not be able to deal with your friend's success. Again, the friendship would not withstand the test.

In most cases, if you stop long enough to see the situation from your friend's perspective, you can have compassion for your friend and forgive him. Often, your friend realizes his mistake and is truly sorry for hurting you. He just doesn't know how to repair the break. Thus you must take the first step.

It takes a great person to be forgiving. When you are willing to forgive, you too will receive divine forgiveness. A friend has weaknesses just like the rest of us do. The songwriter understood this when he penned the song, "No, not one. There's not a friend like the lowly Jesus, no, not one. None else could heal all our soul's diseases." The fourth verse says, "Did ever saint find this friend forsake him? Or sinner find that He would not take him? No, not one." Jesus is the only friend who will never fail you. Because He will never fail you, He wants you to forgive your friend. One day you will need your friend's forgiveness too.

Chapter 16

Forgiving Those From a Different Race

When the final curtain of life falls, will history record that the single cause of the most bloodshed on the face of the earth was racial conflict? I cannot remember visiting a country whose history did not contain some sort of racial conflict. Every nation has had its share of racial problems that have instigated wars and resulted in bloodshed. Often those who tell you of their history do so with an air of pride, as if there would be little left to say without the conflicts.

When we speak of *race*, I am sure different definitions come to mind. One definition can be based on the environment in which we were raised. I was born and raised in Guyana (formerly British Guiana), and I was taught that my country was the land of six

Forgiveness: The Key to Divine Release

races: Europeans, Blacks, Indians, Chinese, Amerindians, and Portuguese. In my mind, all Europeans were one race, as were all Blacks, Indians, Chinese, and Amerindians.

I could not quite understand the difference between the Portuguese and Europeans, but it never became a major issue in my community because all the store proprietors were Portuguese and all the sugar estate managers were considered Europeans. As I grew older I tried to imagine what made the country of Portugal different since it was on the continent of Europe. Occasionally I would try to figure out the difference between the two types of people, but in the end I accepted what I was taught.

Since you may not be as confused or concerned about the definition of race as I am, I hope you will bear with me. My purpose is to reach some level of common agreement and understanding so we can deal with the issue. For the purpose of our discussion, I will use two acceptable reference standards, the *Encyclopedia Americana* and the *World Book Dictionary*. The *Encyclopedia Americana* states that *race* can be identified in every species, which includes human beings. It is of interest to note that humans are a single species, but are identified as various races with genetic characteristics, particularly the color of their skin or some other obvious physical characteristic.

"It should be stressed that it is not the uniformity with which an inherited characteristic appears in a population, but rather its comparative frequency, that serves in defining a population as a racial group. It is important to recognize that racial characterizations are statistical descriptions of the same species differing from each other with respect to certain inherited traits."[1]

The study of human racial population was first carried out by Swedish biologist Carolus Linnaeus. He started this study for three reasons: (a) to recognize and classify racial groups; (b) to understand the origin of each group; and (c) to establish the differences between the racial groups. Examples of racial groups according to the encyclopedia are the Australoid race from Australia, North American Black race, African Black race, South American Black race, and Mongoloid race. The Mongoloid race has five groups: (a) North Chinese; (b) Classic Mongoloid, which is found in a combination of Mongolia, Korea, Japan, and parts of Siberia; (c) South and East Asian—Southern China and Southeast Asia; (d) Tibetan; and (e) the American Indian groups. The American Indian group is further divided into the indigenous groups of the Americans: (a) Eskimo; (b) North American Indian; and (c) South American Indian.

1. *Encyclopedia Americana*, Vol. 23, Grolier Incorporated, 1986.

Forgiveness: The Key to Divine Release

Europeans are divided into four racial groups; Africans are divided into four groups; and Indians (of India) into two groups. Space does not permit me to list all the sub-groups included in the encyclopedia listing.

I do not know the real motive behind Mr. Linnaeus' desire to recognize and classify human racial groups. Maybe his desire was pure; perhaps he simply thought it would be interesting to study and understand the mystery behind people groups. He may even have wanted to explore, to some degree, the greatness of the creator God, who has created all people groups. Or was he simply speaking of the race to which all men belong—the human race?

The *World Book Dictionary's* definition impresses me. It says this: "Race: Any one of the major divisions of mankind, each having distinctive physical characteristics and a common ancestry. White race, the yellow race. The whole concept of race, as it is traditionally defined, may be profoundly modified or even dropped altogether, once the genetic approach has been fully exploited." A second definition is this: "A group of persons connected by common descent or origin, e.g., the Nordic race. We were two daughters of one race."[2]

Gilbert K. Chesterton, in considering race, showed his humor when he identified "human beings as a

---

2. *World Book Dictionary*, p. 1717.

group to which many of my readers belong." I would have welcomed the opportunity to ask Mr. Chesterton to which group he belonged just to confirm that we are speaking of the same group. Was he speaking of the Caucasians or Caucasoids from Northwest Europe or Northeast Europe? Was he speaking of the same group from the Alpine region in eastern France and the Balkans? Perhaps he was referring to the Mediterranean group of Whites, which includes both sides of the sea and extends as far east as Arabia and Iran.

We may never find out which race Gilbert K. Chesterton claims as his own. Was he referring to the pigmentation of his skin, or to humans as a species? All I know for sure is less blood might have been shed if all men had realized that we all belong to the same race. We would also have avoided all of the loathing and bitterness that surround the racial issue. In the end, humans would be less accountable to God for those they have failed to forgive, for less forgiveness would have been required.

With Cain's murder of Abel, we have the first division of mankind—the godly race and the ungodly race. The godly race and the ungodly race continued as two separate races until the godly race, who lived on the mountain, began to lust after the ungodly race, who lived in the valley. They decided to end their lives of separation under God and joined themselves with the ungodly race. Eventually they were completely intermingled and, with the exception of

Forgiveness: The Key to Divine Release

Noah, God could not find a family that was on His side. Everyone was corrupt, thus forcing God to judge the world and destroy the whole human race, except Noah and his family.

After the flood, God started again with Noah, his wife, his sons, and their wives. Once again, He had one godly race. Unfortunately that lasted only a short time and soon the ungodly races reappeared.

*And the sons of Noah, that went forth of the ark, were Shem, and Ham, and Japheth: and Ham is the father of Canaan. These are the three sons of Noah: and of them was the **whole** earth overspread. And Noah began to be an husbandman, and he planted a vineyard: and he drank of the wine, and was drunken; and he was uncovered within his tent. And Ham, the father of Canaan, saw the nakedness of his father, and told his two brethren without. And Shem and Japheth took a garment, and laid it upon both their shoulders, and went backward, and covered the nakedness of their father; and their faces were backward, and they saw not their father's nakedness. And Noah awoke from his wine, and knew what his younger son had done unto him. And he said, Cursed be Canaan; a servant of servants shall he be unto his brethren* (Genesis 9:18-25).

From the three sons of Noah, the whole earth was populated. Ham's son Canaan, and his descendants, received the judgment of his father for looking upon

Forgiving Those From a Different Race

Noah's nakedness. This caused the groups to separate into those who honored God and those who did not. This separation will continue until the new heaven and the new earth appear, wherein will dwell only righteousness (see Rev. 21).

Although these people were separated spiritually, they lived together in the land of Shinar. One day they decided to build a tower to reach up to heaven and to make a name for themselves. The building of the Tower of Babel was in disobedience to God's covenant with Noah, so God came down to see what was going on among the people. After He saw what the people were doing, He decided to confound their language so they could not understand one another. Then the Lord scattered them abroad over all the face of the earth. (See Genesis 11:1-9.)

Once God confounded the language of man, the division became more defined. No longer could they communicate freely, thus preventing them from living together in relative ease. Until Babel, the whole human race spoke one language and was a united, mighty force. They were so mighty that God said nothing was impossible to men and women as long as they put their heads together. Once man could not understand his brother, trust disappeared and suspicion and war became man's pastime. (The devil will always find work for idle hands to do.)

Man fought for territory and power. Each race wanted to control the others for his own security. It was easier for one group to prey on another since the bond of speech was neutralized. Race was determined by language. Those who spoke the same language understood each other and functioned as a group, defending the group against the others. By the time Abraham lived, mankind was once again totally corrupt. To try and correct this condition, God devised a plan to use the ungodly race to reestablish a godly race. He found a man named Abram and called him to follow and obey Him.

Abram obeyed the voice of God and moved from Haran to Canaan. Genesis 14 tells us how nations waged war against one another with the victors dividing the spoils. This type of behavior is what caused Lot (Abram's nephew) to be taken captive from Sodom. Man and his behavior have not gotten better, but worse.

Although we can't be sure where each of the peoples eventually settled, it appears that the descendants of Japheth went to the North (Europe), the descendants of Ham settled in the land of Canaan (Palestine) and Africa, and the descendants of Shem journeyed into Arabia and to the East.

God used these three sons of Noah to populate the whole earth and in His design, planned for the human race to be different in color of skin, design of face, type of hair, height, and size. He did not design us to be different spiritually; nor did He intend for us to hate and take advantage of each other. God intends for all people to live as brothers because we are indeed the children of three brothers. God's plan included a people who would be uniquely different, but one in spirit. Just like the flowers He created, God made some people lighter in complexion, some translucent, some alabaster white, some light brown, and some black.

Blacks and Racial Prejudice

The hate existing in the hearts of men and women of one race against the people of another race allows them to justify and give expression to their anger. Such hate emanates from our failure to discover the common thread that makes each group a part of every other group. Atrocities of one race against another merely because of skin color reflect our failure to restore the bond that existed thousands of years ago.

Most of the unforgiveness and hate that exists between Blacks and Caucasians is the result of Europe's plundering of Africa. I believe history will bear out this truth. As I have grown older, I have learned how to deal with the anger of my youth. It is true that Black people are a despised people in the world today. I do not write for self-pity or to incite further hatred. I simply want all people to realize that we are all related by blood. When we hurt each other, we hurt ourselves.

Before I outline some of the atrocities committed by Caucasians against Blacks, I ask you to remember what I referred to earlier in the Introduction.

Forgiveness: The Key to Divine Release

True forgiveness is to first know what act was committed, by whom and against whom. The Bible says, "Therefore if thou bring thy gift to the altar, and there rememberest that thy brother hath ought against thee; leave there thy gift before the altar, and go thy way; first be reconciled to thy brother..." (Mt. 5:23-24) It is clear then that we must first know what sins we are forgiving.

Before Blacks suffered in North America, they suffered in Africa, Portugal, and throughout the world. According to the writings of Dr. Kwame Nkrumah in his book, *The Challenge of the Congo*, Africans remained on the African continent and carried on their own life style, culture, and religion until 1482. In some parts of Africa, like the Congo, they lived under a feudal system. In other parts they were well-organized economically, politically, and militarily. One such country, Ghana, was well organized. The people in Ghana controlled their own destiny, freely trading with other nations.

Unfortunately, the last King of the Congo had some problems. He existed in a life-and-death struggle with his vassal lords. The situation was so inflammatory that when the Portuguese visited, they were welcomed as potential allies. The king viewed a pact with Portugal as a way to improve his situation. He saw his country enjoying the advancements of the Portuguese, while the Portuguese wanted to bring their brand of Christianity to the Congo. Each side had their own selfish interest in the other's potential.

Forgiving Those From a Different Race

An agreement was made and by 1490 the first shipment of technical aid was received. It included skilled craftsmen and tools, a variety of religious artifacts, and a number of priests. It was the beginning of a trade route, but it would soon result in the dehumanizing of God's creation. One good thing that did come to the Congo was the printing press. Other important advances included foreign exchange, merchant ships, ship-building and navigational equipment, and professionals in medicine and education. In the short-term, it was good for the Congo. What they did not realize was the Portuguese were not so concerned with short-term Christianity as much as long-term control of the Congo and the countries throughout Africa. With their large merchant fleet, they saw the opportunity to accomplish just that.

Jesus taught of wolves coming in sheep's clothing—and this is what the Portuguese turned out to be. They not only signed an agreement with King Mani of the Congo, they also made an alliance with Lord Proprietor, who ruled the Islands of Sao Tome. (The Islands were strategically located off the coast of West Africa.) Mr. Proprietor wanted the blood of our brothers and sisters while the Portuguese wanted to control the ocean. He also acted as a conduit to help the Portuguese export slaves from the Congo.

The following is a summary of the agreement between King Mani of the Congo, whose name was changed by the Portuguese to Don Alfonso after he became a Christian.

Forgiveness: The Key to Divine Release

The Regimento of 1512 provided that the Portuguese should help the King of the Congo in organizing his kingdom. The Portuguese were to introduce a system of European law and to train the Congolese Army in their methods of warfare. They were to teach the royal court to observe correct etiquette, build churches, and provide missionaries.

In return, King Mani was to fill the Portuguese ships with valuable cargo. The Regimento was delivered to King Mani by the Portuguese Ambassador. In the Ambassador's letter of instruction, he was commanded to impress upon King Mani the need to fulfill the selfish desires of the Portuguese.

An extract from the letter of instruction to the Portuguese Ambassador is as follows:

"This expedition was costly so it seemed it would be unreasonable to send it home with empty hands. Although our principal wish is to serve God and the pleasure of the King of the Congo, nonetheless, you will make him understand as though speaking in our name, what he should do to fill the ships, whether with slaves or copper or ivory."[3]

King Mani of the Congo accepted the agreement and provided the Portuguese with the first shipment of human cargo—320 slaves. It was the beginning of

3.   Kwame Nkrumah, *Challenge of the Congo*, New York: International Publishers, 1967, 1969, 1970, p. 3.

Forgiving Those From a Different Race

one of the greatest tragedies to be perpetrated against the Black people. King Mani made an agreement that he lived to regret. Here is an excerpt of the letter he wrote to the King of Portugal:

> "We cannot reckon how great the damage is, since the above-mentioned merchants daily seize our subjects, sons of the land and sons of our noblemen and vassals and our relatives. Thieves and men of evil conscience take them because they wish to possess the things and wares of this Kingdom. They grab them and cause them to be sold, and so great, Sir, is their corruption and licentiousness that our country is being utterly depopulated. And to avoid them, we need from your Kingdom no other than priests and people to teach in schools, and no other goods but wine and flour for the holy sacrament. That is why we beg of Your Highness to help and assist us in this matter, commanding your subjects in the future that they should send neither merchants nor wares because it is our will that in these Kingdoms of the Congo there should not be any trade in slaves nor market for slaves."[4]

This letter was written in 1526, 14 years after King Mani had accepted the Regimento agreement from the King of Portugal. By that time it was too late to change the fate of the people. The traders

---

4. Nkrumah, *Challenge of the Congo*, pp. 3-4.

Forgiveness: The Key to Divine Release

from Sao Tome, the two Islands ruled by Lord Proprietor, had already secured the allegiance of King Mani's vassals or lords. These vassals saw no difference between what the king had done and their capturing defenseless relatives for Lord Proprietor. It was only a case of who was paying more for their services. So they sold their brothers and sisters to the highest bidder. The Portuguese took them to Brazil and the Lord Proprietor sold them on the open market.

The hideous crime against Blacks became so terrible that in the year 1778, 104,000 slaves were exported from Africa. A third of them came from the Congo and Angola. This quote from the Belgian Handbook of the Congo, published in 1959, describes the situation:

> "By the end of the 17th century, the slave trade which had started as a Portuguese monopoly, had become a gigantic international undertaking. The places where slaves were kept became more and more numerous and profitable. The French appeared and turned the Portuguese away from the Port of Cabinda and installed their slave markets. Chiefly beyond the north bank of the river toward Loand and Malemba, while the English traded in the Eastern section."[5]

5. Nkrumah, *Challenge of the Congo*, p. 4.

The world saw Black people as a source of exploitation. Take a look at what King Leopold II of Belgium wrote around 1870:

> "Since history teaches that colonies are useful, that they play a great part in that which make up power and prosperity of States, let us strive to get one in our turn. Before pronouncing in favor of this or that system, let us see where there are unoccupied lands, where are to be found peoples to civilize, to lead to progress in every sense, meanwhile assuring ourselves new revenues, to our middle classes the employment which they seek, to our army a little activity, and to Belgium as a whole the opportunity to prove to the world that it also is an imperial people capable of dominating and enlightening others."[6]

Leopold's ambition became a reality through the Berlin Conference, which met from November 1884 to February 1885. The agreement signed by the nations present gave Leopold personal control of the Congo with the stipulation that it be opened to trade with all participants at the conference. By then, some 15 million of our brothers and sisters from the Congo had been shipped away from their homeland. From that number, about two thirds died enroute due to harsh conditions and terrible treatment.

6.   Nkrumah, *Challenge of the Congo*, p. 5.

Forgiveness: The Key to Divine Release

In 1991, I made my first trip to Ghana on the West Coast of Africa. I was invited to speak at a convention in the City of Takoradi, the second largest city in the country. As I was travelling with the overseer, I expressed my desire to get some information on the slave trade. He told me that the road we were on would take us past Cape Coast, which was one of the main ports for the exportation of slaves.

About two hours later we arrived at Cape Coast and I was taken on a tour. What I observed was quite shocking to me. On the top floor of the fort was a church and the governor's residence. Downstairs were two holding pens, one for men and the other for women. For years a question had preyed on my mind, "How could the Europeans leave Europe and go to Africa and take away our people?" It was on this tour that I found the answer to this question.

The Europeans paid Blacks to capture their own people for a meager sum. When they were delivered to the slave masters, they were placed in holding pens. The pens that held the men could hold up to 200 men if they were forced to stand. The pens were dark and the only light seeped through a small window less than one square foot in size. The men were held for a month to demoralize them. Then they were taken, one by one, to the ship and placed in the hold.

The women were treated a little differently. They had more room, including a courtyard just below one of the governor's patios. The courtyard served two purposes. The women got sunshine and fresh air, and

Forgiving Those From a Different Race

the governor had an opportunity to select the one he wanted for the evening.

My people were treated worse than cattle, and I was angry at what I saw. But who was I to direct my anger toward? I could not make up my mind so I asked the tour guide. He replied, "We did it to ourselves." I agreed with his answer. I could direct my anger at God and at the Europeans, or I could be angry at the Blacks who participated in this atrocity. Even Jesus was treated equally as bad as our ancestors and He, unlike them, did nothing to deserve it.

On the other hand, to some degree we deserved what we got. It is clear from the Scriptures that the gospel came to Africa before it went to Europe. Acts 8:26-39 tells us of the conversion of the Ethiopian eunuch. Acts 13:1 tells us that the church at Antioch had two elders from Africa. Paul did not start his missionary journeys until Acts 16.

God is not unrighteous. I firmly believe that if our forefathers had honored God, they would never have fallen into slavery. It is when people forsake the Lord that judgment follows. The Negro spirituals are a clear indication that Africans knew about God, but failed to walk with Him. Proverbs 14:34 says, "Righteousness exalteth a nation: but sin is a reproach to any people."

God cannot lie—we must face the truth. I have to agree with one Black author who in his autobiography said that he would rather be in America and go

Forgiveness: The Key to Divine Release

back to help Africa than to be in Africa wanting to come to America. America is blessed, but when a nation forgets God, judgment follows. God has not forgotten the evils of America, and we can only stay His hand of judgment by learning to forgive each other.

Other Racial Issues

I am sure that every race or group of people can speak of the injustice that was meted out to them. In 1967, I went to a seminar in West Berlin. While I was there, I was taken on a tour to visit sites used to house and, ultimately, exterminate the Jews. My wife and I were also privileged to visit the museum of the holocaust in Jerusalem that depicts the genocide that took place in Germany. The scenes brought tears to my wife's eyes. I could go on and on. What about the peoples of Yugoslavia, of Lebanon, and of those in the Palestinian situation? Everyone has suffered in some form or fashion because of the color of their skin, including the Amerindians, American Indians, and Carib Indians. Who has taken up the cause of the Amerindians, whether American or Carib?

There is a great evil under the sun in the United States of America—this evil is racism. Someone has said that the time of greatest division in the world is in America at 11:00 a.m. on Sunday morning. The Blacks go to the Black churches and Whites go to the Caucasian churches. Yes, there are a few exceptions, but very few.

Forgiving Those From a Different Race

The Caucasian groups of North America have spent centuries trying to justify the evils of slavery. They desperately try to convince themselves that Blacks, as a race, are less human than Whites. They try to convince themselves that they were not sinning when they held slaves legally. Nevertheless, after the abolishing of physical slavery, the nation continues to practice social, mental, and spiritual slavery. This practice has become so ingrained in this nation, like other nations, that everything we do reflects racial lines.

I happen to be a member of one of the larger Pentecostal Christian organizations in America. This organization has sent out missionaries around the world to preach the gospel of Jesus Christ. I hasten to add, thank God they did and continue to do so. I was blessed to sit under the ministry of those who were sent to Guyana. We have been fortunate to maintain our relationship over the years. Our friendship is genuine; we sleep in each other's homes and preach for each other. We are real friends, buddies, if you will. I am sure there are others who can make similar statements. Unfortunately, these are not the norm, but rather isolated cases.

There is a very good friend and colleague of mine from Guyana. We grew up in the same organization. She went to Bible school and was one of the first graduates of the school. She continued her studies, completed her first degree, and for many years served the school as its president. Finally, she felt

Forgiveness: The Key to Divine Release

the call of God to continue her studies in the ministry. So she came to this country to attend the seminary of the organization that taught us all of our lives. Initially, they rejected her. God overruled them and she was accepted on a trial basis. She subsequently disappointed those who believe Blacks are of a lesser species than Caucasians.

She completed the divinity program and received her Master of Divinity. During her time at our seminary, she endured snide remarks and innuendos, but her performance was amazing. She even was asked to accept dorm rooms that Whites did not want.

Later she shared this interesting event with me. During her practicum she was given a class at one of the local grammar schools. At one of her teaching sessions, a Caucasian student from another class was passing her room and heard her teaching. The student stopped and listened long enough to be captivated by the lesson, remaining until it was over. Suddenly, the girl became upset. After some time my friend succeeded in calming her. Then she asked the girl what the source of her reaction was. She could hardly believe what she heard. The girl said her parents taught her that Black people are not intelligent enough to teach her, but here she was listening to a Black teacher.

I was invited to my friend's graduation. I felt honored to be included and gladly accepted the invitation. My wife and I headed to the school for the ceremony and while there we toured the organization

Forgiving Those From a Different Race

headquarters. I was surprised that I did not see one Black person at work at our headquarters. Maybe there are some, but if there were, they all took off that day.

Another example of the evil of racial division involves a cousin of mine. She graduated from one of our colleges and felt the call of God on her life to serve in the mission field. When she applied, she was rejected by the Mission Board. They claimed they could not send out single women. I think they should have added "Black" single women, because the church I pastor supports a single Caucasian woman who is a missionary. Still, I was pleasantly surprised to meet the first Black missionary from my organization when I visited Jamaica in October, 1993.

I am sure there are many unbiased people in my organization who would like to see changes made. Many have seen the need to confront the evil of racism in the Body of Christ in this country and others. For example, the director of our home missions has demonstrated a heart for all the souls of America. He made this known in his address at our General Council in Portland, Oregon, in August of 1991. Since then I have spoken to him when he visited us in New York. I believe that he sees the need for a true confrontation on the state of our church.

We must recognize our sin against each other based on the color of our skin and, by the power of the Holy Spirit, remove the walls built up over the centuries. As happened to the Berlin wall, let us

Forgiveness: The Key to Divine Release

start breaking down the wall of racial prejudices so the Holy Spirit can move freely within all people groups. I remember the fear that came over me when I first went through checkpoint Charlie from West Berlin to East Berlin in 1967. I also remember the difference in the atmosphere when I visited again 25 years later. I was free to travel from East to West or West to East. The wall was gone and all the barriers were removed.

I truly forgive all Caucasians even as Christ has forgiven me. It is my prayer that all races confront racism for what it is, an evil under the sun, and forgive those who have trespassed. Only through this forgiveness can we find forgiveness from our heavenly Father. Then, and only then, will the Holy Spirit be free to move among us to end the division.

The federal government legislated busing to change racism in our schools, but they do not have the authority to legislate the Church. I pray they never will have that authority. The Holy Spirit can, as the song says, "do it again." When the Holy Spirit was moving in the early Church, He broke down the wall of racism. He raised up a church at Antioch that was racially integrated.

Now there were in the church that was at Antioch certain prophets and teachers; as Barnabas, and Simeon that was called Niger, and Lucius of Cyrene, and Manaen, which had been brought up with Herod the tetrarch, and Saul (Acts 13:1).

Forgiving Those From a Different Race

Both Jews and Gentiles were prophets in this first church of Antioch, and from this church the Holy Spirit sent out missionaries.

My organization has accomplished a lot for God. It is time for those things accomplished abroad to begin to take place here in the "good ol' U.S. of A." I beg the leaders of all Christian denominations who are called to be shepherds to the pastors, to seek the Lord for a genuine love for Blacks in this country and to change policies that exclude Blacks from participating at various levels and in various ministries.

When you check the number of Black ministers in my organization, if you are honest, you will see that the majority are from outside the USA. Those who have come are accepted to a degree, while those from the United States are rejected. The question is, "Why can American missionaries go overseas to train and educate Blacks, who in turn can come to a strange land and make it, but the Blacks right here are denied the opportunity?"

If we, as a Christian Pentecostal organization, really want to see a change in our inner cities and especially among Blacks, we must confront the error of deciding the fate of a man or woman based upon skin color.

In Korea, we boast of one of the largest churches in that nation. What God is doing in Korea, He can do right here in the United States. Why is it that the

Forgiveness: The Key to Divine Release

Church in America is struggling, while overseas God is pouring out His Spirit? We cannot live on what used to be. God is the God of the now. We don't need to leave America and go to Korea as many are inclined to do. We need to bring the Spirit from Korea and make it happen here.

My fellow brethren, I speak from my heart. I cannot see myself as a member of any other Christian group. I thank God for raising up this organization, but let us not miss the day of our visitation. The apostle Paul said that though he had preached to others, he himself could have become a castaway. You have preached to me in Guyana and my understanding of the Scriptures was a result of your missionaries. I have grown to love you because you taught me that "Jesus loves the little children, all the children of the world. Red and yellow, black and white, they are precious in His sight." If these words are true, let us remember what James said: "My brethren, have not the faith of our Lord Jesus Christ, the Lord of glory, with respect of persons" (Jas. 2:1). He goes on to explain that treating people based on the external is doing just that.

Let us remember this: "And [God] hath made of one blood all nations of men for to dwell on all the face of the earth, and hath determined the times before appointed, and the bounds of their habitation" (Acts 17:26).

Chapter 17

The Right Choice

When we speak of forgiveness, we should think of one very important truth in Scripture. The one word that I believe best exemplifies truth, is the word *all*. Paul writes, "For all have sinned, and come short of the glory of God" (Rom. 3:23). I recommend that you meditate on this verse and let it speak to you. Everyone who has been born of woman, every person on planet Earth, has sinned. That includes you and me. You too have sinned and come short of the glory of God and, therefore, are in need of forgiveness.

That old cliché about glass houses in effect says, "Do not throw stones at someone else's house if you too have a glass house." This is the reason God has said, "If you are not willing to forgive others, you yourself cannot receive forgiveness." The time has

Forgiveness: The Key to Divine Release

come for you to cease looking for reasons not to forgive. Your experiences of hurt may vary from the situations described in this book; nevertheless, they are not beyond God's ability to heal. You simply must want the healing process to begin. You have the key to unlock Heaven's healing stream to you. You open that flow when you decide to forgive the individual who has hurt you so badly—be it father, mother, brother, sister, friend, pastor, church member, teacher, boss, or any other person.

Every person, regardless of his or her position or relationship to us, is a human being. As humans, it is possible to err or rub someone the wrong way. Our strength in God is manifested, though, when we learn to forgive those who have wronged us. Relationship or skin color makes no difference. God made all men of one blood to dwell on the face of the earth. Every human being has similar tendencies to love, hate, forgive, or not forgive. The ability to choose is a right which God has bestowed on every person, and He will never take away this right while we are in this human state.

Forgiveness is a choice you must make. The decision to forgive is important for your own survival—spiritually, socially, emotionally, and physically. Joshua knew the power of choice. He knew that his people's survival depended on the choice the people made—whether to serve the Lord God who brought

The Right Choice

them out from the land of Egypt and the house of bondage; or to serve the gods of wood and stone, the gods of the other nations.

Now therefore fear the Lord, and serve Him in sincerity and in truth: and put away the gods which your fathers served on the other side of the flood, and in Egypt; and serve ye the Lord. And if it seem evil unto you to serve the Lord, choose you this day whom ye will serve; whether the gods which your fathers served that were on the other side of the flood, or the gods of the Amorites, in whose land ye dwell: but as for me and my house, we will serve the Lord. And the people answered and said, God forbid that we should forsake the Lord, to serve other gods. For the Lord our God, He it is that brought us up and our fathers out of the land of Egypt, from the house of bondage, and which did those great signs in our sight, and preserved us in all the way wherein we went, and among all the people through whom we passed (Joshua 24:14-17).

Unfortunately, Israel did not realize how serious the wrong choice would be until after Joshua's death. Joshua laid a clear path before them and challenged his people to choose life. It was Jehovah who brought them out. It was Jehovah who was responsible for their freedom and for bringing them into a good land flowing with milk and honey. His people were powerless against the Egyptians and would have remained

Forgiveness: The Key to Divine Release

in bondage if God had not come down to deliver them. Joshua had no doubt about the true and living God. He knew God's ways are just and true, that His ways are best for people in every dimension of life.

Spiritual Bondage—In Egypt, they cried day and night for deliverance from the bondage of other gods. Jehovah was the only God who had a plan of deliverance. It is in keeping with His righteousness, love, and forgiveness that He brought them out to be a people unto Himself. Forgiveness is the basis of His relationship with man. Whenever you refuse to forgive, you put yourself into bondage spiritually because you cut yourself off from your heavenly Father.

Physical Bondage—Physically, it has been proven that unforgiveness can cause a person to develop a nervous stomach and even ulcers. One colleague told me his personal experience with unforgiveness. One of his family members had committed an act that hurt him very much. He was not willing to forgive her right away; he was too disappointed with her. He carried his hurt until one day his whole body broke out with a terrible condition, forcing him to seek help from his doctor. To his amazement, after the doctor completed the examination, he said to my colleague, "Sir, for this condition, if I had come down with it, I would have needed to see a person in your profession to help me overcome this sickness." My friend stared in amazement as the doctor continued, "Sir, something is on

The Right Choice

your mind that you need to get rid of. There is no medication that I can give or recommend that will help you. You must release whatever is on your mind."

Emotional Bondage—Emotionally, unforgiveness produces tension between two people. From my own experience, I can testify that I became tense toward my children when things were not right between us. Many times I had accused them unjustly before I had all the facts. It is for this reason Jesus said that if you have anything—any suspicion—against anyone, to go to that person and confront the issue. You may be judging someone wrongfully, and then your attitude toward that person would always be wrong. Forgiveness brings freedom to relate to one another.

Social Bondage—Socially, unforgiveness has placed people on a social island. Some years ago I was invited to visit the home of a very attractive lady. Her home was lovely. One of her sisters was sick and she was staying with her, so they invited me to pray for her healing. I arrived there with some of the members of my congregation and in the group was another of her sisters. As we entered the home we felt the tension, but did not know what was happening. Sometime later I asked the sister, who is a member of our church, about her sister whose home we visited. To my surprise I learned that even though they are from a large family, no one has been in touch

Forgiveness: The Key to Divine Release

with this sister because if someone rubs her the wrong way, that one is ostracized for life. She was not willing to forgive.

Psychological Bondage—Psychologically, unforgiveness can result in wrong thinking toward a person. It is possible for a person to make an honest mistake and not really intend to hurt you. Until you deal with the problem, you will never know it was a mistake. A few years ago I decided it was time to have the interior of our home painted, so I called someone to do the job. In the process of moving things around, the painter broke one of my wife's figurines. It was a valuable piece from the Lladro line of angels. When she discovered it, she was very upset and wanted me to get the man to replace it. I was ignorant of the value of such things and decided to let it go. She kept on confronting me about it—and rightly so—but because of my lack of knowledge concerning those things, I have not spoken to the man to this day. In 1993 I wanted to do something special with her and planned a trip to Spain. I was not aware that I was taking her to the home of the figurine manufacturer. During our time there, I discovered that my lack of knowledge had caused me to misunderstand my wife's concern. Even though she had confronted me, it resulted in further hurt. She may have assumed I was not concerned about her feelings. I did care, but I had not seen the reason for her hurt. I only understood her side when we went to Spain and I saw the cost of her Lladro pieces.

Any wrong thoughts you have can lead to wrong actions because you may not know all the reasons surrounding a person's response. Learn to forgive and let the Lord handle it. He knows exactly what caused the situation. People do not always hurt each other because of evil intent; sometimes things happen within the best of intentions. So leave your hurt with the Lord.

David understood the way the Lord could look into a situation. He said:

O Lord, Thou hast searched me, and known me. Thou knowst my downsitting and mine uprising, Thou understandest my thought afar off. Thou compassest my path and my lying down, and art acquainted with all my ways. For there is not a word in my tongue, but, lo, O Lord, Thou knowest it altogether. Thou hast beset me behind and before, and laid Thine hand upon me. Such knowledge is too wonderful for me; it is high, I cannot attain unto it. Whither shall I go from Thy spirit? or whither shall I flee from Thy presence? If I ascend up into heaven, Thou art there: if I make my bed in hell, behold, Thou art there. If I take the wings of the morning, and dwell in the uttermost parts of the sea; even there shall Thy hand lead me, and Thy right hand shall hold me (Psalm 139:1-10).

Forgiveness: The Key to Divine Release

I suggest that you read and meditate on Psalm 139 in its entirety. After reading and meditating on it, I trust you will be convinced that the One who commanded us to forgive those who wronged us, knows what is good for all of us. I hope that you will begin today to make a list of all the people toward whom you feel hurt. Take that list and begin to confront each situation prayerfully and, as God leads you, make contact with the people involved. Let them know you are sorry for what happened between you and them and tell them you forgive them.

Jesus forgave those who crucified Him and prayed that His Father would forgive them too. Jesus, who did not hurt anyone, forgave everyone. Even so, we who have hurt so many must learn to forgive all others their trespasses.

NOTES

NOTES

NOTES

NOTES

NOTES

NOTES

NOTES

NOTES

NOTES

NOTES